Cheese Balls for Jesus

*Funny, Faith-Filled Stories
to Encourage and Inspire*

MOLLY SANBORN

10:31 PRESS

10:31 Press
Minneapolis, MN

Library of Congress Cataloging-in-Publication Data
Sanborn, Molly.
Cheese balls for Jesus: funny, faith-filled stories to encourage and inspire/ by Molly Sanborn.—First edition.

FIRST EDITION

Cover and interior design: Purpose Design
Cover photo: Mandy Benson
Back cover photo: Alison Lea Photography
Speaker booking page photo: Bobeedy Photography

What People are Saying about Cheese Balls for Jesus

"Molly Sanborn is a wonderful storyteller! Taking Jesus (but not herself) seriously, she invites the reader into her most embarrassing moments and messy situations. By the end of this engaging book, you will feel you have found a new friend."

—**Josh D. McDowell,** author

"Leave it up to God to use a backpack of cheese balls to draw people to Cheesus—I mean Jesus! Molly Sanborn masterfully combines comedy and conviction, humor and heartache, wit and wisdom as she intertwines Scripture with her amazing God stories."

—**Steve Saint**, missionary, author, son of martyr, Nate Saint

"I love *Cheese Balls for Jesus*! Molly is an authentic, hilarious, and insightful author. She made me laugh out loud and inspired me to look for more creative ways to lighten up and live! Don't hesitate to take notes as you read, recording the moments your eyes are opened to the unique ways God can use you to share His love with others. If God can use the Cheese Ball Chick, He can certainly use you!"

—**Ken Davis**, author, speaker,
Founder of Scorre™ Speaker Training

"There is nothing that we love more than a great God story. And this book is full of them. God is always at work and is always inviting us into His story. You will laugh, and you will cry at how God has worked in amazing ways in Molly's life. And He wants to do the same in yours. So, buckle up and prepare for the ride of your life!"

—**Dave & Ann Wilson**, Co-hosts of *FamilyLife Today*

"I couldn't put it down! Molly Sanborn is *seriously* crazy, funny, transparent, and vulnerable, while simultaneously loving and talking about Jesus. If you don't know Jesus Christ, you'll love seeing Him in action through this collection of true stories. *Cheese Balls for Jesus* is about relationships and how lives can be transformed if we allow people to see a loving reflection of Jesus through us!"

—**Dr. Clarence Shuler**, President/CEO of BLR: Building Lasting Relationships, author of *Finding Hope in a Dark Place*

"Molly is an incredible communicator both on stage and on paper. Molly's God stories will inspire and encourage you to notice where God has been working in your life. Her passion for Jesus and her love for others comes through on every page. If you like to be encouraged and want to draw closer to Jesus, look no further. I highly recommend *Cheese Balls for Jesus!*"

—**Greg Speck**, youth and family communicator, author

"It's not often I come across a book that is equally suited for both teenagers and adults. Students today hunger for adults to be authentic and vulnerable. Adults today need to be reminded that God is at work in their lives. *Cheese Balls for Jesus* is a beautiful mix of fun and depth. Whether you're 14, 40, or 84, this book should be in your hands!"

—**Heather Flies**, Junior High Pastor at Wooddale Church, author, student communicator

"Molly's stories are engaging and inspiring, and her real-life persona, the Cheese Ball Chick, is laughable and lovable. Over and over again, God is the one who takes center stage as Molly shares her stories with vulnerability and humility. Whether she is teaching youth to "Keep Your Pants On" or drawing a spiritual parallel to the time her pants almost cost her life (read chapter 7!), her God stories will leave you wanting more!"

—**Mark Bjorlo**, President of Converge North Central

"A mentor once told me, 'Never stop telling what God has done for you or there will come a day that you doubt it ever happened yourself.' Molly's fun and faith-filled book of God stories will encourage every reader and remind them that God loves to use anything, even cheese balls, to bring Him glory. *Cheese Balls for Jesus* will have us all writing down our own testimonies and crazy adventures to encourage and inspire others. There is great comfort and confidence in remembering what God has done for us! You won't soon forget Molly's inspirational stories."

—**Daniel Gil**, author, speaker, Champion of *American Ninja Warrior*, Season 12

"Molly Sanborn is one of our best camp speakers, in large part because she makes it as much of a priority to connect with the campers when she is not on stage as when she is on stage. Through making personal connections and handing out cheese balls, Molly really cares about our campers. *Cheese Balls for Jesus* is no different. You will feel like you're hanging out with Molly. She has great stories, great focus, and it's all wrapped up in the understanding that Molly really cares about you and your walk with Jesus!"

—**James Rock**, Director of Trout Lake Camps

"This book is SO good! Molly has been speaking at our camp for over twenty years, and I never tire of hearing her stories of God's faithfulness. For years, I have been wishing I could share her stories with others, and now I can! This book is a timely reminder that we have a God who loves us so much (and wants us to laugh too!). I highly recommend *Cheese Balls for Jesus* for all ages and stages of life!"

—**Camie Treptau**, Director of Village Creek Bible Camp

"'When I'm laughing, I'm listening,' said one of our staff after hearing Molly speak at our women's retreat. Whether speaking or writing, Molly uses humor to reach the hearts of her audience. She doesn't shy away from the hurt and heartache and can somehow make you laugh and cry at the same time! Our women love her and keep demanding we bring her back year after year!"

—**Steve Pinkley**, Executive Director of Hidden Acres Christian Center

"Molly Sanborn is, by far, the best speaker and author I've ever been married to!"

—**Craig Sanborn**, Director of Student Ministries, Converge North Central, speaker, extraordinary husband to the Cheese Ball Chick

A Note from Molly

I'M SO EXCITED you are reading this sentence! Thank you. Now you've read three. That means you're reading my book, and you're reading the intro nonetheless! Impressive. You could have skipped to the first chapter, but here you are. I'll try to make it worth your while!

Many times over the years, I've been asked, "When are you going to write a book?" My answer has always been the same—only when I confidently know the Lord is calling me to do so. What a waste of time it would be without His equipping, guidance, and blessing!

In your hands (or on the screen) is a compilation of what I call "God stories." Each chapter represents a monumental moment in my life where I have seen God show up in undeniable ways. No wonder God gave me the green light on this book—the stories make Him look pretty good—which He totally is!

I've been sharing these stories from stage and over coffee with friends for years. Recently, while recounting a few of them with a friend, she interrupted me with a question, "Molly, why do you have so many cool stories with God?"

As I took a minute to ponder, it dawned on me. "I think it may be because I tell people," I said. "Each time I see God show up, I don't shut up! Maybe God is motivated to do cool things in my life because He knows I'm going to tell people how awesome He is."

Words from David in Psalm 40:8-10 come to my mind. "I desire to do Your will, my God; Your law is within my heart. I proclaim Your saving acts in the great assembly; I do not seal my lips, Lord, as You know. I do not hide Your righteousness in my heart; I speak of Your faithfulness and Your saving help. I do not conceal Your love and Your faithfulness from the great assembly."

Why do I have so many God stories? This is what I've experienced: The more I pray, the more I find myself waiting and watching for clear answers, and the more answered prayers I end up noticing! You can't have an *answered* prayer if you don't pray in the first place. Because I pray about almost *everything*—from the seemingly inconsequential and borderline embarrassing to the monumental—at least *some* will surely get answered as expected or even better than expected. And sooner or later, I have enough to make a book out of them!

But please know, there have been plenty of requests I've made to God that have elicited a "no" or a "not yet." More about that at the end. For now, I want to celebrate what He has done and invite you to the party. Some are short stories. Others are longer. Some are heavy on humor while others go deep and make me more vulnerable than I ever thought I'd be in a published book. It may be a bit of an emotional rollercoaster, so buckle up!

Love,

Molly :)

Dedication

To Poppy and Tal.
May you always notice where God is working, and
may you never stop telling people about it!

The Stories

Chapter 1

Cheese Balls for Jesus

Can I get these through security? I wondered. I wasn't trying to smuggle anything *illegal*, after all.

I had just come from a speaking engagement in Virginia Beach, Virginia, where I gave a faith-based version of my "Keep Your Pants On!" message to about 1,000 teens at a Christian conference. Basically, I was encouraging them to make good choices in relationships and to make their most important relationship the one they have with Jesus.

At the end of the weekend, volunteers were cleaning up the speaker and musician's hospitality room, tossing leftovers and empty containers into the trash, but there sat a giant bucket of cheese balls, only partially consumed. One of the volunteers talked about how sad it would be to waste the cheesy goodness and asked if anyone wanted to take them home. I volunteered, not for the snacks, but for the large bucket itself. My sister, a mom of three young boys at the time, had recently asked me to keep my eye out for toy storage containers. Jackpot! The cheese balls wouldn't fit in my luggage, so I tucked them under my arm as I headed to the airport.

Once inside, I noticed quite quickly that people were staring at me. At first, this was okay, because I'm an extrovert and had an unlimited number of smiles to give back. But then, as I was walking down the corridor toward security, I noticed people laughing. *Do I have something in my teeth? Is my fly down? Am I trailing toilet paper behind me?*

As I got in line for the security checkpoint, giggles grew from fellow fliers, conversations ensued, and it seemed that everyone was smiling. I unloaded all my belongings into the bins and watched the cheese balls go into the x-ray machine. I wondered if they would come out the other side or be confiscated.

My cheese balls stalled. The man at the monitor looked puzzled as he tried to make out the image on the screen. When I reunited with my snacks on the other side, there were eight security officers surrounding my cheese balls. *Well, it was fun while it lasted,* I thought.

As I was getting ready to say goodbye to my cheese balls, one of the security officers asked why I had them. *Oh no,* I thought, *now I'm going to be interrogated, or worse, late to my gate!* I couldn't have been more wrong. This jovial group of TSA officers started laughing and cracking jokes. "Did you eat all those yourself?" one asked while eyeing the partially empty container. "You're starting to turn orange," another joked. "I think we're going to need to take these from you ma'am," a kind older gentleman said while winking.

To alleviate the traffic jam I created, I said farewell, tucked the bucket back under my arm, and found my gate. Chuckles continued as the cheese balls and I boarded the plane. I found my aisle seat and placed the large container on my lap, trying to pretend it was completely normal.

The passengers in my row inquired about the cheese balls. "You never know when a craving will come upon you," I joked. Then I said, "Just kidding, I just got them at a conference I was speaking at." When they asked what I was speaking about, I summed it up with one word, "Cheesus, I mean, Jesus."

The flight attendant made an announcement, "Ladies and gentlemen, if any of you are hungry, there is a cheese ball lady with snacks in seat 9D." I was as shocked as everyone else! The flight attendants went on to announce my snacks and me two more times throughout the flight, and everyone laughed and smiled. Neither of my seatmates were phased, and it turned into a significant spiritual conversation during our flight to Chicago. *Cheese balls to Jesus in less than ten seconds!* I mused.

As I trekked across the Chicago O'Hare terminal to my final flight home, multiple people called out to me with greetings like, "Hey, Cheese Ball Lady!" "Cheese Ball Girl!" "Hey, Cheese Ball Chick!" Another person thanked me for making them smile. *Wow!* I thought. *Traveling has never been so much fun!*

While waiting to board the plane home, my cheese balls *again* instigated an introduction. A college-age girl made a comment about them, and the next thing I knew, we were talking about God! She was looking for a church in Minneapolis, so I invited her to mine. (And she came!)

Soon after my cheese balls' maiden voyage, I told some friends about the experience and how the bucket of snacks brought the world together—well, at least a few flights and the airports in between. One of my friends said, "You should carry cheese balls around and make people smile–see how God uses it." This challenge was intriguing, and I've never been one to turn down a dare. *However,* I thought, *lugging a huge container around might affect basic daily functioning. Somehow, I'd need to be hands free.* I thought.

And then it hit me—a bus. Sorry, I couldn't resist. A thought hit me—a thought. If I could just create some sort of way to carry it around, maybe like a backpack, then I could be hands free. I turned to good 'ole duct tape to get the job done and fashioned a harness to hold the bucket.

I'll never forget walking into a mall with my friend, Katie, by my side and a giant bucket of cheese balls on my back. I really didn't know what would happen and didn't have any sort of plan, except to try *not* to act weird. Too late? Perhaps.

But if we gauge the success of our first public appearance on smiles, laughter, and conversations, I'd say my cheese balls and I got an A+! I learned right away not to approach people, but rather to let them come to me. There is a fine line between creepy and unique, and I try to go with the latter.

The people came, but...they didn't eat. They were incredibly curious about my contraption but cautious about sticking their hands in a big container, likely contaminated by who knows how many hands before them.

That's when I decided I needed to create a sanitary dispensing system—one where folks can eat cheese balls germ free. I enlisted my older brother, Andy, and we began to brainstorm. We held our planning session in the PVC pipe aisle of Home Depot. Just as we were feeling stumped, Jim, donning an orange apron and a bushy beard, asked if we needed assistance. I think he was just hungry for cheese balls, which of course I was willing to provide!

Roping Jim into our shenanigans was the best decision we made that day. Not willing to fail a customer or get stumped on a project, Jim continued to help us even *after* he clocked out. He even utilized table saws and tools to make my dream a reality.

I walked out of Home Depot that day with the first-ever (and only that I know of) cheese ball dispenser. And since then, it's been attached to almost 200 different containers and has traveled to thirty-four states, seven countries, and counting.

I wore it on my first date with my husband. I wore it as a contestant on the ABC TV show, *Wipeout*, in 2011. I tried to wear it skydiving, but my guide recommended I wear a parachute instead. It's been strapped to my back while skiing, biking, roller-skating, and cruising around on my scooter. I love to pass bikers on their big motorcycles and imagine their response when they see my orange backpack whiz by. Recently, I pulled up to a stoplight on my scooter and asked the tattooed couple on the Harley Davidson next to me if they wanted to race. We revved our engines, and I left them in the dust—for about two seconds.

I've worn my cheese balls to weddings (including my own!), restaurants, movies, plays, concerts, and sporting events. For the first five years, my cheese ball backpack was an extra appendage—going *everywhere* with me.

Once I became a mom, I couldn't wear it *all* the time since I had a little more to carry around like bottles, diapers, wipes, pacifiers, extra clothes, toys … oh, and my baby! Speaking of my baby–I wore my cheese balls to the hospital on delivery day and handed them out to nurses and doctors. Word got around and hospital staff started visiting my room for snacks and smiles!

There have been countless encounters where my cheese balls have paved the way to bring encouragement and joy. They seem to magically break down boundaries and disregard demographics. I've been approached by *all* kinds of people while wearing my cheese balls.

I'll never forget the group of grunge teen girls at the mall. Pierced, tattooed, and wearing tattered jeans, they passed me with no more than a glance, followed by a double take to see what big orange thing I had on my back. Usually that would be weird for people to stare at my backside, but under these circumstances, it was acceptable.

Upon hearing their giggles, I turned and smiled with a little wave. They did the same, and the next thing you know, we were talking and laughing, giving a new meaning to cheesy smiles! We visited for so long that the mall security guard had to close down our conversation...but not before he accepted our offering of cheese balls.

The girls happily agreed to take a picture for my new social media page, and we said farewell. A few days later I received a call from my friend, Stacy, who had seen my post. With excitement in her voice, she told me she was the school counselor for one of the girls named Helen, and she had been praying that she would find a mentor. By the time she called me, she had already cleared the consents, and Helen was anxiously awaiting my answer. I'm pretty sure I said yes before she finished asking me to meet with her!

Stacy got us officially paired up, and our first time hanging out was anything but awkward. Our encounter in the mall had broken the ice, and we felt like old friends. In fact, during our first meeting at a coffee shop, I stole away to the bathroom just so I could send my hubby a quick text telling him how well it was going and how much I was enjoying meeting with Helen. When I returned to the table, Helen had a grin on her face and showed me the text on her phone. Oops, I accidentally sent it to her! I thought, *Well, at least now she knows how I feel about her!*

Helen and I continued to meet for several years until I married and moved away. And thanks to this book, we got back in touch. To think it all started with a backpack of cheese balls!

After that first experience flying home from Virginia, the cheese balls have gone with me on almost every trip—and that's a *lot* of flights. It's no small sacrifice to fly with them because they count as my personal item! Who needs ChapStick, a wallet, and a water bottle anyway?

As I step from the jetway through the plane door, I always smile at the flight attendants who are there to welcome me onboard. Just before their eyes turn to the next passenger, I make a sharp right turn which brings my backpack into their line of sight. As I begin maneuvering down the tiny aisle and listen to their laughter, I turn around and say with a smile, "I'll be in seat (whatever my seat number is) if you are hungry." I can always count on giggles, curious questions, and sometimes an invitation to meet the pilot. One time I was even invited to move from my cheap economy seat to comfort plus just because I was wearing snacks on my back!

While traveling home from speaking at school assemblies in Ohio, I experienced some flight attendants who were especially interested in my orange carry-on. After the usual smiles and giggles near the cockpit, I headed for the back of the plane. By the time I reached my seat, I'd made eye contact with nearly every passenger and exchanged about as many smiles. Just after reaching cruising altitude, I relaxed into my seat and wondered how soon they'd start the snack service. Little did I know that *I* would be the snack service that day! Two flight attendants approached me and asked if I would be willing to go up and down the aisle to offer cheese balls to everyone. "We'll follow you with water," they said as if it had already been decided.

I thought they were joking, but they waited until I got up. They kept their word and literally followed me up and down the aisle as I dispensed my cheesy snacks. To my surprise, most people happily stuck their hands out to grab a portion. One girl emptied out her Pringles can and asked me to fill her container!

There was only one grumpy person on the whole flight, and guess who he was sitting next to. Yup. Me! He was on the aisle, so I had to squeeze past him multiple times throughout the flight as people called, "Hey, Cheese Ball Chick."

After we landed, I said farewell to the pleasant plane of passengers (minus one) and headed for my connecting flight. While waiting for a shuttle, a timid, petite woman approached me. She was so soft spoken that I could hardly hear her. I leaned in to hear her say, "Thank you so much for bringing the cheese balls on the flight today."

"You're welcome!" I replied. "So glad you enjoyed eating them."

"No, actually, I didn't have any, but I watched you in amazement as you went back and forth to passengers." Now I'm thinking she was either really bored or her screen was broken, and even though she didn't eat cheese balls, I provided some entertainment during her flight.

The sweet lady continued, "My family and I are returning from my Aunt Lillian's funeral."

"Oh, I'm so sorry to hear that." I empathized.

I realized she must have appreciated the distraction from her sadness. Nope. She went on, "My aunt had a special tradition every time we visited. She would buy a special treat—the same special treat each time—and have it sitting on her kitchen table when we arrived. It was a giant container of cheese balls. And now, here *you* are on *our* flight home, handing them out!"

Tears filled her eyes (and mine!) as we took in the truth that this was *not* a coincidence. I had such confidence that this was God's kindness and compassion on display. I had to make sure she saw it too. I told her that there is a God who sees her, knows her, and wants to comfort her. He is not too distant or busy to see her sadness and orchestrate such an encounter to bring joy to her heart.

Speaking of encounters, remember my encounter with Home Depot Jim? Little did he know that he would have a verse in the Cheese Ball Song (find it on YouTube) dedicated to him. And little did we both know that over a decade later, we'd still be friends—and not just on Facebook. My husband, Craig, and I invited him to our wedding, and he's been to our house for dinner multiple times. Just last month, we met for impromptu pie at Perkins—

well, *I* had French Silk pie and Jim had a hearty breakfast. We caught up on life, reminisced about the day we met in March of 2008, and talked about spiritual things. I admire Jim for his diligence in searching for the truth. He's read countless books and studied all kinds of religions. I couldn't help but think of (and share) Jeremiah 29:13 that says, "You will seek Me and find Me when you search for Me with all your heart." I encouraged Jim to pray and talk to God about his questions. I have no doubt that God will make things clear to Jim as he seeks Him.

I also have no doubt that God gave me the cheese ball idea for a greater purpose than I could have ever imagined. What started as a silly little dare to "bring joy to the world one cheese ball at a time" has led to countless encouraging conversations and opportunities to pray for people, remind them of their worth, and point them to Jesus.

I know this is cheesy (c'mon—I had to!) but I wear cheese balls for Jesus. All these fun and faith-filled encounters are because God chose to *use* cheese balls as a way to point to Him. These incidents, which are anything but coincidence, can be summed up by 1 Corinthians 10:31. "Whether you eat or drink or whatever you do, do it all for the glory of God."

Did you notice it says, "whatever you do?" Besides sin, I can't think of anything that wouldn't fit in the category of "whatever." I wear cheese balls for the glory of God and to encourage others. What can you do for the glory of God that will fan the faith of those around you? Do you have a special talent, interest, or hobby? Do you play a sport or an instrument? Are you into theater or performing? Do you sing, dance, write, paint, draw, sew, or craft? Do you excel at academics? Can you teach? Can you build things? Can you fix things? Are you good at crunching numbers (or cheese balls)? Ha!

Whatever you do—it matters! God can and will use *you* to encourage others and impact eternity *if* you offer yourself and your talents up to Him.

> **God's Word says...** "God has given each of you a gift from His great variety of spiritual gifts. Use them well to serve one another. Do you have the gift of speaking? Then speak as though God Himself were speaking through you. Do you have the gift of helping others? Do it with all the strength and energy that God supplies. Then everything you do will bring glory to God through Jesus Christ. All glory and power to Him forever and ever! Amen." (1 Peter 4:10-11 NLT)

Let's Talk to God...

Dear Lord,

Thank You for giving me gifts and talents and creating me with unique passions. Thank You that You want to use me and my life to bring glory to Your name. Please reveal to me specific ways in which I can be a bright light for You and draw others to You. *Amen.*

It's Your Turn!

What are some of your gifts, talents, passions, or even quirks?

How could they be used to point others to Jesus?

Chapter 2

A Midnight Mission

I'LL NEVER FORGET hearing the news. My older (and only) sister, Rachel, announced that she was pregnant with her husband Tim. Wait. No. That doesn't sound right. She and her husband *together* were pregnant with a baby. Phew. Glad I straightened that out! Anyway, this was exciting news because it would mean that I was on my way to acquiring the title of Aunt Molly!

I was thrilled and didn't think it was too much to ask if I could be in the delivery room on this monumental day. Clearly, it was too much to ask. I received a big fat NO. Speaking of No, "No-No," as I like to call my nephew, Nolan, was born without my presence on April 26th, 2001. I can only imagine how much better his life would be if I had been there for him during the trauma of birth. Okay, enough drama. Nolan has turned out to be a young man of superior quality.

Before Nolan reached two years old, his parents announced that they were pregnant again. *Yes!* I thought. *Now they will for*

15

sure let me be in the delivery room since I've proven myself to be a great aunt. No, not that kind of great aunt (I was too young for that!), but rather an incredibly loving, attentive, fun, funny, amazing, kind, and generous aunt. After rattling off my credentials, I was shocked to receive *another* No from Rachel and Tim. In fact, this time, I think they said, "NO WAY."

Nine months later, my nephew, Adam, was born. Surprisingly, he also seemed to thrive even though I wasn't his first point of contact in this world. I was starting to lose hope when Rachel and Tim announced they were pregnant *again! Third time's a charm*, I thought, *or will it be three strikes and I'm out?* I had to find out. This time, I approached much more tentatively, bracing myself for certain rejection. And that's just what I got.

A few weeks later, just when I had finally given up (I hate to admit that I did), Rachel and Tim approached me with a proposal. They told me, "Molly, you can be in the delivery room," (insert jumping, shouting, hugging, weeping tears of joy) "but..." they continued. *Wait! There's a but!?! No, no, no. But what?* "...but only if the baby comes on your birthday, October 11th."
Their baby's due date (October 3rd) was eight days before my birthday. Oops. Retract premature celebration from the record.

While my joy deflated just a tad, I was still thrilled that there was now a possibility that I would witness (from a very far distance of course) the miracle of birth. I immediately sprang into action. I laid my hands on my sister's tiny baby bump, prayed, and coached the baby through a detailed escape plan. "On October 11ᵗʰ, which is a great day to be born—actually, it's the only day to be born—just head down please!"

The most important action I took, and why this story gets to be in this book, is that I prayed. While I prayed more fervently for "bigger" requests, I did not neglect this one. In fact, I prayed quite faithfully about it. I happen to believe that God is not only interested in the monumental moments and dire decisions of our lives, but the day-to-day desires of our hearts as well.

So, for the following months of Rachel's pregnancy, I made sure God knew about this desire! I would also remind the baby of the plan each time I saw my sister. As her belly grew, so did my anticipation. But that excitement came to a screeching halt when I got the call on September 30ᵗʰ that Rachel was in the hospital, ready to deliver.

Well, *she* was ready, but turns out the baby was *not*. "Thank you, Jesus!" I yelled, as my poor sister begged the Lord for this baby to be born.

As October came, and the due date blew by, I found myself really believing this was going to happen. Rachel was quite uncomfortable, and by this point was probably regretting her little arrangement with me as it seemed God may be in on the plan.

It was Sunday, October 10ᵗʰ, 2004. I didn't even try to contain my excitement. I started visualizing the next day, but not too much visualization. Remember, I just wanted a bird's-eye view, maybe even a bird-with-one-eye-closed view. Then I realized that my entire day from 9 a.m. until 9 p.m. was totally booked! From college classes to volleyball practice, to coaching, there was no time for me to squeeze in a trip to the hospital!

So, I took my prayers to the next level. I once heard that if we want God to answer specifically, then we need to pray specifically. So that's what I did. I asked the Lord for the baby to be born in the middle of the night—close to midnight if possible. I didn't tell anyone that prayer, but I thought I'd help the Lord out and get labor started. But how on earth does one actually do that? I wasn't sure, so I asked Google!

A simple search of "how to induce labor" led me to some very weird practices, some involving rare spices from the other side of the world. I sorted through the jungle of information and learned that physical activity can help. While some of the "physical activity" suggested was not at all in my department (yikes!), I figured a brisk walk might get contractions going. I called Rachel and asked if she was willing to allow me to try some of the suggested tips for inducing labor. "As long as it doesn't hurt," she answered.

Armed with a rolling pin, octopus-shaped head massager, and exercise disc, I drove twenty minutes to their house. After some dance moves on the swivel disc, Rachel allowed me to gently attempt to "roll the baby out of her belly" with the rolling pin and use the head massager on her stomach. If not to induce labor, it worked to elicit a couple giggles, which I read could also help. Next, around 8 p.m., we set out on a walk. We didn't even make it halfway around the block when she doubled over in pain.

"Yes!" I screamed.

"No!" Rachel wailed.

"This hurts!" Rachel added. It was the first contraction, and they only got stronger and more frequent as we walked. Back at her house, I sat next to the couch as my sister sprawled out in pain. With a stopwatch in hand, I timed the contractions.

Around 9:30 p.m., the contractions had not yet reached the point that would warrant a trip to the hospital. Rachel gently reminded me that she's been through false labor before, and this was probably the same thing. She wanted to go to bed and promised to call if anything changed. I drove back home to my parents' house with a perma-grin. The worship music was blaring, and I was celebrating early.

I couldn't sleep and neither could my parents who would need to babysit the older boys if this turned out to be the real deal. I lost track of time as I sat at the table doing homework. I was jolted to alertness when I heard the phone ring. My dad answered, looked at me with a big smile, then looked at the clock, and mouthed, "Get going." It was EXACTLY 12 a.m., and my midnight mission had begun!

I dashed to my car and made a pit stop at the gas station for an extra-large cappuccino. I felt like a VIP when I checked in at the front desk of the hospital. As I approached the room, I wondered how my sister and brother-in-law would receive me. Would they regret they made this deal? Would I feel welcome?

Rachel and Tim couldn't have been more gracious. How sweet of them to share this moment with me. I found a nice chair tucked away—way away—in the corner. This would be my home base. I had no plan of leaving this safe space until my new niece or nephew was born *and* cleaned up. I didn't feel it necessary to be up close and personal.

As the contractions grew closer together, they also grew more intense. The moaning and groaning and occasional shrieks left me looking like a wide-eyed hoot owl in the corner. When my sister was told to push, I closed my eyes and gritted my teeth. I was listening intently for the cry of a baby, but instead heard the nurse yell, "Sister, sister, come hold her leg!" My eyes popped open, and with my head on a swivel, I searched the room for a nun. Surely, she wasn't talking to me!

She was talking to me.

I cautiously approached what looked like a battle zone. My eyes were squinted just enough to identify and grab a hold of my sister's leg. *What is happening?* I thought. *This was not part of the deal.* But here I was, just inches and minutes from meeting the guest of honor. Minutes dragged on as my sister struggled and struggled to get this baby out. Everything else seemed to come out—yes, I mean everything!

At this stage in my life, I was primarily an abstinence speaker, sharing my "Keep Your Pants On!" message in schools and churches across the country. And at this stage in the night, I was convinced I was going to be abstinent for life! As I dodged fluids and listened to my suffering sister, I daydreamed of adopting a nice clean baby someday.

My attempt at dissociation was interrupted when the doctor whipped out what looked like a sophisticated toilet plunger. He suctioned this vacuum contraption to the top of the baby's head and pulled like a world-class, tug-of-war champion.

While the baby put on a good fight, the doctor came away with the gold medal as he showcased the messy bundle of a baby boy. I'm not sure if my nephew was crying for joy to be out, or embarrassment due to his cone-shaped head. Regardless, I thought he was perfect—goop and all.

I gave the proud parents some time alone with their son as I retreated back to my corner. I couldn't help but shake my head in amazement at God's sweet birthday gift. He not only answered my prayer, but He went above and beyond, as is His nature, and allowed me to experience this sacred moment to the max. He saw to it that I would be a part of the very first contraction all the way until my sweet nephew, Daniel, made his debut—on our shared birthday, October 11th! As unprepared as I was for the front row seat, I wouldn't change it at all!

To this day, Daniel and I have a super special bond. Now well into his teen years, we still celebrate each birthday with a date while donning our matching birthday boy and birthday girl hats—the same ones I bought for his first birthday. We call each other B² (B-Squared) which stands for "Birthday Buddy." We've even created a special handshake.

When I look at Daniel, I am reminded that I have a God that not only shuts the mouths of lions and performs mighty miracles, but also sees and listens to my silly little desires. And rather than dismissing them, He takes great delight in fulfilling them.

age 4

age 5

age 10

age 9

age 11

age 12

age 13

age 17

God delights to fulfill your desires. Is there something in your life that matters to you that you haven't yet talked to God about? Maybe you've held back because you think it is too small or too silly. I encourage you to take some time to be honest with God about your hopes and dreams—big and little. Doing so doesn't mean He'll always answer as we hope, but without an ask, there can't be an answer.

God's Word says... "Keep on asking, and you will receive what you ask for. Keep on seeking, and you will find. Keep on knocking, and the door will be opened to you. For everyone who asks, receives. Everyone who seeks, finds. And to everyone who knocks, the door will be opened. You parents—if your children ask for a loaf of bread, do you give them a stone instead? Or if they ask for a fish, do you give them a snake? Of course not! So if you sinful people know how to give good gifts to your children, how much more will your heavenly Father give good gifts to those who ask Him." (Matthew 7:7-11 NLT)

Let's Talk to God...

Dear Lord,

Thank You for being a God who cares about the little things. Thank You for Your invitation to pray about everything and ask about anything. Please help me trust You with the big things and the little things in life, and give me faith to believe that You hear and want to give me good gifts. *Amen.*

It's Your Turn!

List some of your heart's desires—big and small, serious and seemingly insignificant.

_____

_____

_____

_____

_____

_____

_____

_____

Now take some time to talk with God about each one of them.

Chapter 3

Flirty Gertie

I WAS STRANDED on the corner of Penn and 42nd Avenue in Minneapolis, Minnesota. Quite unlike myself, I had arrived at the bus stop *early*. I couldn't risk missing the bus that was going to take me to my brand-new job at Olive Garden. (I'm so sorry, I know. Now I've elicited a craving for buttered bread sticks and unlimited soup and salad.)

But there I was, sitting, waiting, well past the time the bus was scheduled to come. Time was ticking, and I *had* to get there. If this bus didn't come within five minutes, I'd be late and would likely be fired. I had no cell phone, so my only option of calling for help was to God. And that's just what I did. I asked Him to get me a ride to work.

I even gave Him some ideas. Maybe a friend or a relative could just happen to drive by. Maybe the bus could actually come. Maybe a police officer could escort me. However, I had not committed any crimes, so that option was unlikely. I considered pulling out my thumb to hitchhike, and then remembered I was on a busy city street and not a quaint country road. That was not such a great idea.

Dejected and with no bench on which to rest, I found myself squatting in the dirt among cigarette butts and trash. My Olive Garden tie dangled in the debris. Just as I was giving up hope, an old Buick pulled up to the stoplight. My eyes met those of a kind, elderly woman. Her hands were meticulously stationed at 10 and 2 o'clock on the steering wheel, and she sat upright and alert. Her head was like a bobblehead as she looked at me, then the stoplight, then back again. This went on for what felt like five minutes.

Seconds before the light turned green, she reached over, and with all her might, manually rolled down the passenger side window. "Honey, do you need a ride?" she said in the cutest, thickest German accent. "Yes!" I said as I simultaneously deemed her a safe stranger. With no time to spare, I ran to her car with my tie flapping in the wind.

The kind woman introduced herself as Gertrude but gave me permission to call her Gertie. She told me she lived on Russell Avenue and was heading to the Brookdale Mall for errands, so she could take me that far. *That will get me closer to work but not quite close enough,* I thought. Still, this was better than sitting in the dirt!

Wanting to make Gertie feel comfortable, I told her that I went to church on Russell Avenue. Her hands left the steering wheel, and her eyes left the road. We nearly caused a crash. "Honey!" Gertie exclaimed, "I go to church on Russell Avenue too!" When we realized we went to the same church, she immediately insisted that she drive me all the way to Olive Garden. Forget her errands, Gertie's new mission was getting me to my job on time!

For the next ten minutes, Gertie interrogated me about my family, my background, and my life. I didn't get to learn much about her, but I knew I liked her, and this would not be the last time I saw her. Little did I know just how *much* I would see her from that point forward.

I gave her a big hug and wasn't quick enough to dodge her wet kiss. I thanked her profusely for getting me to work on time and practically danced into Olive Garden, full of faith and excitement. I ran to the first person I saw, which happened to be the bartender. I didn't even know his name, and I'm pretty sure he didn't know mine, but that didn't stop me from launching into a super speedy version of what just happened. I told him how I prayed and how God answered. I couldn't contain my joy, and he must have been drawn to its source inside me—Jesus.

My co-worker, whose name I found out was Nick, said, "Wow, if being a Christian is like that, I think I want to know more."

Nick came to church with me that Sunday and for many Sundays after that. My dad met with and mentored him for six months! The story *could* stop there, and it would be worth writing about, but it gets better!

Remember Gertie? Well, I found her at church and began sitting next to her. That led to Sunday afternoon meals, which led to mid-week meals and more. I preferred going out because I quickly discovered that nearly *every* food item in Gertie's tiny house was expired. I'll never forget the night I tried to quench my thirst with a tall glass of chocolate milk. I'm not sure why I didn't notice the curds kerplunking into my glass, but believe me, I noticed the texture (and taste) when it reached my mouth! I was basically drinking chocolate cottage cheese. I spewed it into Gertie's sink as discreetly as possible and committed to check expiration dates from that day forward.

When we did go out, Gertie was a hoot. Once she took me to a German restaurant and unashamedly flirted with the server to get more meat. That's when I gave her the nickname, "Flirty Gertie." She and I had fun driving around town in my convertible. We were six decades different in age, but that didn't stop us from painting the town red.

Some of my best highlights with Gertie were our sleepovers. I was a little shocked when she brought out her silk pajamas for me to wear. I showed her the pair I had brought, but she insisted. She wanted us to match—her in pink and me in green. What a sight we were! The first night I slept over, I was left staring at the ceiling and listening to Gertie snore. She apparently went to bed *very* early. So, the next time, I came prepared with Tylenol PM. It must have worked because the next morning, I woke up with Gertie's face about one inch above mine. She let out a sigh of relief when I opened my eyes. She exclaimed, "Oh honey! I thought you were dead!" We laughed!

As Gertie and I continued our friendship, she joined me in praying for my future husband. When I finally met Craig at age twenty-six, she did not take it easy on him. After an interview and some obvious winks from her to me, she sealed her approval with a double pinch of Craig's cheeks. Upper, not lower. She wasn't *that* flirtatious!

Because Gertie had no children of her own, Craig and I felt it would be special to have her play the role of Honorary Grandmother at our wedding. She was so excited but also concerned she may not make it that long since she was getting up there in years. Gertie held on and walked so tall and proud as she was escorted down the aisle, wearing her special corsage. She was especially thrilled to see her name in our wedding program.

Gertie passed away not long after we were married, and I had the honor of sharing at her funeral. I told the story of how we met and reflected on many of our special memories. When I prayed that afternoon on the corner of Penn and 42nd Avenue, all I was asking for was a ride to work. But instead, God brought me Flirty Gertie and a fabulous friendship. It all started with a simple prayer, yet God took it and turned it into something I could never have imagined or even would have thought to pray for.

That's what He does. And that's what He wants to do in Your life. He wants to take your ordinary and make it extraordinary.

God's Word says..."Now to Him who is able to do immeasurably more than all we ask or imagine, according to His power that is at work within us, to Him be glory in the church and in Christ Jesus throughout all generations, for ever and ever!" (Ephesians 3:20-21)

Let's Talk to God...

Lord,

Thank You for being a God who exceeds expectations. Thank You for having bigger and better plans for my life than I do. Please help me trust You with all parts of my dreams and disappointments, knowing You see the big picture. *Amen.*

It's Your Turn!

Can you recall a time in your life when God came through in a surprising way and exceeded your expectations? (If you find yourself staring blankly at this page, ask God to reveal where He has shown up in the past and where He is working now.)

_____

_____

_____

_____

_____

_____

_____

_____

Now take time to thank Him for it (and tell someone else!).

Chapter 4

Gravity or Gabriel?

I WAS YOUNG AND IN LOVE. Well, I was in love with the *idea* of being in love. There was no man in my life, besides God. I was in my early twenties, and at my sister Rachel's house, I noticed a sticky note exchange on the counter between her and her husband, Tim. I snooped on the mushy-gushy messages (don't tell them!), and found myself thinking *Oh, I can't wait until I can do that with a guy someday!*

And then I got an idea. Actually, I can't take credit for the idea. I think it was that man in my life I mentioned earlier—God. He speaks in a still, small voice, almost like a thought that pops into your head. He whispered the words, "You don't need to wait to write notes of appreciation. How about you write a sticky note of praise to Me each day?"

I didn't think it was a good idea to turn down the God of the Universe, so starting that night, I wrote a daily note. I put the date in the top right corner of the square sticky note and wrote one or two words or a short sentence of gratitude. Wow. It got addicting—fast. Who knew that counting your blessings could make you feel so good?

"Snowflakes" "Otters" "Rainbows" "Waterfalls" "Clouds that make shapes" "Seashells have holes" "Fireflies—bugs whose abdomens light up!" (True Story: It's their tummies not their tushes. My son, Tal, wanted you to know that.) "Taste buds" "Riding my scooter" "Sun gives natural highlights" (Thrifty gals like me really appreciate saving money at the hair salon!) "For keeping me safe when I fainted during my haircut" (You'll get to hear that whole story in a future chapter—so stay tuned!)

I just wrote down whatever came to mind, and eventually I found myself noticing things all day long. No longer was I just thankful during the ten seconds it took me to write my daily sticky note, but I developed an attitude of gratitude all day long.

This was an incredible habit to build, especially to be utilized in trying times. After a few years of doing this, my room was plastered with praises from floor to ceiling. It became an impromptu worship space for visitors as I watched my friends come in and immediately start reading my notes. Sometimes I had to pull them away from the notes to hang out with me!

My colorful collection started to get cramped as I could hardly find any free space for my next notes. I did manage to squeeze in "Gravity" one day—March 4, 2004, to be exact. I wrote, "Gravity—it's nice we don't just float away!" I stuck it among the hundreds of other praises.

A little over a week later, I was in my room and noticed one sticky note had fallen to the ground. As my knees dropped to the ground to pick it up, so did my jaw. It said "Gravity!" There were literally hundreds of other notes that *could* have fallen, but no—it was this one. I immediately penned my next note, "The Gravity sticky note fell! Ha! Ha! You [God] have a sense of humor!"

> March 14, 04
> The GRAVITY Sticky note fell!
> Ha! Ha! You have a sense of humor! :)

I can just see it. God calls the angel, Gabriel, over and says "See Molly's room down there? See the "Gravity" sticky note? Your mission is to get that one—just that one—on the floor."

Whether it played out like that or not, I am convinced that it was not a coincidence. God had His hand in it. He creates smiles. He crafts laughter. He is the author of joy. He is the original comic. Don't believe me? Have you seen some of the animals He created?

I have moved several times since putting all those notes up on my wall. I now contain them in a treasure box because it reminds me of Matthew 6:21. "Where your treasure is, there your heart will be also." As I have taken the time to treasure thankfulness, my heart has grown full of gratitude.

So how about you? If your heart was put on a scale that weighed grumpy to grateful, where would the needle point? Regardless of the results, here's some great news. With simple and intentional acts, you can grow gratitude.

Grab a pack of sticky notes or start a list in a journal or on your phone. Or how about write daily gratitude posts on social media?

> **God's Word says...** "I will give thanks to You, Lord, with all my heart; I will tell of all Your wonderful deeds." (Psalm 9:1)

Let's Talk to God...

Thank You, Lord, for Your goodness to me. Please open my eyes to see all Your blessings and help me take every opportunity to tell of Your wonderful deeds. *Amen.*

It's Your Turn!

Well, what are you waiting for? Tell God what you're grateful for!

Chapter 5

Overwhelmed to Overflowing

I USUALLY WEAR A SMILE, but there was a season when it was hard to put it on. But I'm getting ahead of myself. Let's start at the very beginning, a very good place to start. (Sorry, I got us singing "Do-Re-Mi" from *The Sound of Music* now.) Okay, I remember a floating sensation, some muffled voices, darkness, and extremely cramped quarters. And what was that long cord attached to my belly button? I digress. I guess we don't need to start that far back. The beginning of this particular story is actually the ending of a different story of my life: college. I had just graduated with a degree in Elementary Education, but my real passion was in speaking, and I knew it.

I had been volunteering the previous few years as an abstinence speaker for a crisis pregnancy center. They would send me into public schools to talk to health classes on this touchy topic. This is where I developed and honed my "Keep Your Pants On!" talk. After a while, word got around, and churches started inviting me to speak to their youth groups. Then camps called me. Eventually I was speaking multiple times a week, mostly on a volunteer basis.

I absolutely loved it. I felt passionate about it. I even felt God had called me to it, but it was not paying the bills. And now I had a significant college loan to pay off, not to mention rent for my apartment and gas for my car. Oh yeah, and food—I guess I needed to eat.

Well aware of my need for money *and* my call to ministry, my dad approached me with a crazy idea. He proposed that I design and develop a coffee shop in the empty warehouse he and my mom had just purchased. In exchange, they would pay me a small salary and completely pay off my $25,000 loan, *if* and *when* the coffee shop opened. Then I would be released to pursue ministry and speaking, debt free, and we would find someone else to manage and run the coffee shop.

"Is this a joke?" I asked my dad. "I know nothing about business, and I don't drink coffee." He tried to convince me by talking about my creativity and drive, buttering me up by saying he couldn't think of anyone more capable than me. "That's nice, Dad, but I don't think so." He asked me to pray about it, and I hesitantly agreed.

My dad's request came right before I had planned a short solo getaway in northern Minnesota. I set aside time to pray, process, and seek God about my future. As I drove along Lake Superior on Highway 61, I began entertaining thoughts about the coffee shop. *If I opened a coffee shop, which I'm not going to do*, I thought, *I would name it "Overflow."* Not long after this fleeting thought, I made a pit stop at a beautiful waterfall. I hiked quite a bit off the beaten path to find my own little patch of land over-looking Tettegouche Falls. I know, I couldn't pronounce it either.

I sat cross-legged under a tree, Bible in lap, and felt a re-freshing breeze. As I looked down, my eyes instantly fell on one phrase: "my cup overflows." I was staring at Psalm 23, wondering if this was coincidence or confirmation.

For the rest of my trip, I continued to seek God about my fu-ture. He had to have been very patient as I asked again and again what His will was, especially after His pretty obvious answer at Tettewhatever State Park (No offense to the name. I just couldn't pronounce it!). Upon returning home, a family friend introduced us to an incredible woman who had always dreamed of running a coffee shop. Get this—she had a culinary degree *and* a business degree! And she was a Christian! She wanted to work with us and committed to help me get Overflow off the ground, then take over as manager once it opened. This was just what I needed to finally say yes to God.

I was going to open a coffee shop! Oh, it was so fun—at first. I vaguely remember designing a house in home economics class in high school using graph paper and colored pencils. Now I got to do it for real! Since we didn't hire an architect for the floor plan, it was all me.

My favorite design element was a huge, overflowing cup which would sit on a round table in the center of the space. Translating my idea to real life was a bit of a puzzle, however. One night, when I couldn't sleep, I used about 100 manila folders and designed a mock cup to see what size I liked. Finding a sculpture artist to form and cast a piece that was over five feet in diameter *and* incorporate a fountain was a tall order. But God provided, and the final product was truly a work of art!

I felt like a little girl playing house. My cupboards were over-flowing with yummy samples from all kinds of vendors—chocolate biscotti, delicious smoothie mixes, and of course, lots and lots of coffee which scored me brownie points with my friends and family. I still had time to speak, and life was going great.

Until…

Three months into it, I opened our credit card statement. There were over $3,000 of mysterious charges. It didn't take long for me to discover who made them. Remember the capable and equipped woman we had hired to eventually take over the business? I felt sick to my stomach. *What was happening? Why was this happening?* After a very tearful conversation with her, I fired our first and only employee.

To this day, I have no ill will toward her. She told us she had every intention of paying us back, and I believe that she thought she would. However, it was very clear we had to let her go. And in fact, as you will see, I believe God used her absence to do a mighty work in my life. I had been placing my security in her rather than in God.

I had no time for a pity party. We were in full swing of development, and many decisions had to be made every day. Buying an espresso machine is more overwhelming than buying a new car, I decided! I also had to learn to pronounce "espresso" correctly. Apparently, you get judgmental looks from highfalutin' coffee snobs if you say *ex-presso*.

Picking out toilets wasn't easy either! When the contractor asked me what style I wanted, I said, "I don't know, one that flushes?" He wasn't satisfied with that answer, so I went to the hardware store, and like Goldilocks, sat on each one until it felt just right.

I had to choose the bean supplier, the food supplier, the paper supplier, the credit card processing software, the tile, the paint colors, and where the outlets should go. My list of responsibilities was a mile long, and at the same time, I was getting more speaking requests than ever before. They were even paid gigs, but I had to let them fall by the wayside. I didn't have the bandwidth to take them on.

I'll never forget my last speaking event before focusing exclusively and indefinitely on our new coffee shop. After the event, the youth pastor asked why I wasn't speaking full time. I sheepishly admitted that I was opening a coffee shop. This guy had no mercy. He said, "What!? You were made for this. Why on earth are you opening a coffee shop?" At that point, I wasn't so sure myself. I blamed it on God.

Speaking of God, I had been talking to Him a lot. I was pestering Him, actually. I begged God to replace the woman we had to let go. If God could send her, then He could surely send another. I needed help, and I definitely was not *made* to run a coffee shop. We had ads out in newspapers and online, and my parents even hired a professional headhunter. Sounded pretty barbaric to me, but whatever works, I guess!

I offered to God what I thought was a great suggestion. *How about You answer two prayer requests with one answer? This person should be my future husband!* I was twenty-five and single and couldn't think of a better time to meet my knight in shining armor! I didn't see any reason why God couldn't send a handsome (yes please!), coffee-drinking, entrepreneurial, business whiz of a man to announce he was there to rescue me and run the coffee shop!

God didn't like my idea. Bummer.

Just a few months from opening, I got a temporary job at a small neighborhood coffee shop. I needed to learn the ropes since I would be hiring and managing my own staff soon. *Gulp.* Speaking of staff, I realized I needed an application of some sort. So, I Googled "coffee shop applications," found one from a familiar franchise, and changed a few words around. I hope that's legal!

We had an eager bunch of employees but no one to lead them. Oh yeah—me. I forgot that I was the person in charge until we found my replacement. I remember one day getting a fleeting thought that God may, for some crazy reason, allow me to open Overflow by myself.

Unfortunately, I knew a lot of Bible stories in which God seemed to specialize in taking unqualified people and having them do big, seemingly impossible things. Moses led the Israelites out of Egypt. Esther became Queen and freed her people. Daniel faced ferocious lions. Peter walked on water, and the list goes on. I assured God there were enough stories demonstrating

His power through unqualified people, and I didn't need to be one of them.

As deadlines came due and the opening of Overflow drew near, my anxiety increased. I felt way in over my head. I was putting in close to seventy hours a week, which would eventually increase to eighty or more. I was having a hard time sleeping, and when I woke up, I felt like there were a ton of bricks on my chest. Eventually the tears started flowing—I guess you could say they were *overflowing*. I would go to bed crying and wake up crying, with a tiny bit of sleep in between.

I felt physically nauseous from the stress and didn't feel like eating. I lost twenty pounds and literally felt like I was wasting away. My family noticed this too. My little brother, Jeff, basically kidnapped me and took me to a Vietnamese restaurant, which was an interesting choice since I don't even like that food when I'm hungry! He stared at me until I finished my meal and then announced we would be going to Dairy Queen next. I knew things were pretty bad when I couldn't even enjoy a Heath Blizzard with extra Heath.

My sweet, concerned mom packed brown paper sacks with lunches and sent them with my dad to the shop. I didn't always eat what was inside, but I *always* read every word on the outside. My mom wrote Scripture all over the bags, inserting my name in the verses whenever appropriate. To this day, those brown paper bags are one of my most treasured possessions. It was the truth written in black sharpie markers in my mom's handwriting that kept me going.

"Molly, have I not commanded you? Be strong and courageous. Do not be afraid; do not be discouraged, for the Lord your

God will be with you wherever you go." (from Joshua 1:9) Only a mom could be this straightforward: "This is the day the Lord has made. Molly **will** rejoice and be glad in it—whether Molly feels like it or not." (from Psalm 118:24)

As I grew wearier and more overwhelmed, my ability to recognize lies from the enemy was waning. I learned firsthand that when we are emotionally, mentally, and physically drained, we are more susceptible to lies from the enemy. Satan was trying to convince me that I misheard God in the first place, that He didn't *really* call me to do this, therefore, He wasn't going to help me through it. *I will be stuck running this coffee shop forever!* That's when I decided to change the name from Overflow to Overwhelmed. Not really, but it would have been more honest.

My mom modeled the best way to fight those lies—with the truth. So, I turned to the source and wrote out a pep talk for myself. I made myself read it each day before I went to bed and each morning after I woke up. At least half the time, my eyes were blurry with tears as I recited my mantra titled "Truth." Here's a snippet of it:

On September 9th, 2006, I committed to move forward in developing and running Overflow. I made this decision after five months of prayer and seeking advice. Ultimately, I chose to do this because God called me to it, and I went forward only because I knew He would be supporting me, enabling me. I had confidence in this because of the truth I find in Scripture: "For the eyes of the Lord range throughout the earth to strengthen those whose hearts are fully committed to Him." (2 Chronicles 16:9)

Isaiah 41:10 and 13 tells me not to fear because God is with me, strengthening me, helping me, upholding me, and holding my right hand! Isaiah 40:28-31 explains that even though I am weary that God, the Creator of the Universe, does not become tired. He gives strength and power to the weary as we wait on Him.

Many heroes of faith have gone before me and have been tested in much greater things, stretched far beyond, and called to more difficult tasks. They had hope for things they had not yet seen (Hebrews 11). Paul understood that when we are at our weakest point, that is when Christ can be our strength (2 Corinthians 12:9-10).

God, as soon as I woke up today, I was faced with a choice: I could be consumed by the worries and fears that can so easily plague and discourage me, or I could let truth reign and choose to move on, even though I don't know what is ahead nor do I know how to get there. Today, I choose the latter. I choose to follow You because You know where we are going. I choose to hold my fears and anxieties up to You and not allow them to debilitate me. I choose to move on in faith and commit to do the best I know how to do, as unto You, and then trust the outcome to You.

I ask for opportunities to let people know where I am drawing my strength. I ask for the ability to have joy and be able to smile, laugh, and enjoy this day even though it is going to be very hard. I ask for protection from Satan's schemes to bring doubt and trip me up. In the name of Jesus, that sweet, wonderful name, I ask this. I thank You, God, for this opportunity to be stretched and grown in ways I never wanted to be! I thank You for entrusting Overflow to me as Your steward. I thank You for the wisdom and favor You have granted thus far. I thank You for TRUTH. Please help me walk with You in truth and love. I love You God.

I wish I could tell you that reading those words twice each day made me feel better. Most of the time, they didn't. But I *know* they did something *inside* me. God promises that His Word does not return void but will accomplish its purpose (Isaiah 55:11). I turned to the truth not because it made me feel warm and fuzzy, but because I believe God's Word is a lamp to my feet (Psalm 119:105), and I was in the dark!

God's Word also promises wisdom to those who ask (James 1:5). So, I asked—a lot! I memorized James 3:17 that tells me God's wisdom is pure, full of peace, gentle, reasonable, full of mercy and good fruits, unwavering, and without hypocrisy. I ended up applying that verse daily! Through conflicts with staff, contracts with vendors, and daily decisions, God's Word equipped me to walk in wisdom.

However, I began to have a hard time completing my thoughts and sentences. I started to think or say something, but my words were hijacked by a competing thought or task that needed to be done. My head felt like a washing machine over-stuffed with an extra-large load of clothes banging against the sides.

The internal stress manifested itself externally with headaches and tight muscles. My dear friend, Jessica, a massage therapist who lived down the hallway in my apartment, offered massages "on the house" (not on *top* of the house!) during this trying season. I'll never forget one night when she generously hauled her massage table down to my apartment. As I laid on my stomach with my head smushed in the little face hole, I began to cry. My tears hit her feet, and I think there may have been some snot mixed in.

All of a sudden, I felt a few drops of liquid on my shoulders. *Is the apartment above having plumbing issues?* I thought. *Ew, I hope this isn't sewer water!* Oh, no. It was much sweeter than that. It was Jessica's tears. She was crying with me. Until then, I had no idea the power and comfort that could come from someone simply sitting *with* me in my sorrow.

Despite the magnificent massages and doing all the right things—prayer, reading God's Word, reciting Scripture, listening to worship music—I still battled anxiety and sunk into depression. Here's an excerpt from my journal entry on April 27th, 2007:

Hello Lord. God, I have never felt so down, so despondent. I hate to use this word, but—depressed. As much as I don't have experience with depression (Thank You), I think this is how it must feel. Ouch. I don't feel like writing. I really don't feel like doing anything. But I'm making myself write this down because I want to make sure it's documented to me and to others that if Overflow is a success, it's not me. God, I feel so low and burdened, I find myself almost hoping some accident would occur with me so I'm not able to run Overflow. That's crazy, but that's how desperate—how incapable—I feel. It's like I'm shutting down. My face is stern. It's hard to smile. I can't feel happy. I think all I have energy left to say is HELP. —Molly

I remember training staff who I felt were better equipped to train me. I would send them on a break just so I could go in the back room and cry. I kept staring at the front door, waiting for my prince charming to walk in and sweep me off my feet. And maybe he could sweep the floor while he was at it!

But God held back. Overflow opened. I could hardly believe it. We intentionally had a soft opening which means you don't advertise, but just unlock your door and see who wanders in. The hope was that we could ease into it rather than getting inundated with all kinds of customers on the first day. Well, I think someone must have rented a plane to write a sign in the sky.

Overflow was literally overflowing with people on the first day! We ran out of bread for sandwiches. We had a line out the door. Customers were coming back three times in the same day *and* bringing friends with them. Everyone loved Overflow. I loathed Overflow. I even secretly and desperately had prayed that no one would come!

As the week went on, business boomed, and the phone was ringing off the hook. When I recognized the caller ID as a friend or family member, I would answer, "Overwhelmed Espresso Café, how can *you* help *me?*"

One week after opening I was still at the shop long after it closed, trying to make sense of scheduling staff—something I wouldn't wish on anyone! I decided to sleep up in the loft since I'd need to be back at 5 a.m. anyway. After telling my parents my plan, I reluctantly heeded their urging to go home to my own bed. That was divine advice, because in the middle of the night, thieves broke in and stole our safe! Everyone was so happy I had chosen to go home. I felt disappointed I hadn't been there to be stolen away. A change of circumstances would have been nice. Kidding, not kidding.

I remember crying as I was chopping basil for our special mayonnaise recipe. *This batch could be extra salty*, I thought, *if I let my tears drop in the mayo*. Silliness aside, I was in a dark place. I looked at the knife and had thoughts I never thought I would be capable of having. One rainy day while driving back to my apartment, and crying of course, I considered cranking the steering wheel around a turn. *It would look like an accident*, I thought.

I was in a very dark place and needed help. Fortunately, I listened to my parents' prodding and saw a counselor. (If you or someone you love is having suicidal thoughts, you are not alone. Please seek help or reach out to the National Suicide Prevention Lifeline by calling or texting the three-digit number: 988.)

The days dragged on, and I grew more and more depleted. My parents, who saw my disheveled state, made it very clear that

I could bow out at any time. They cared more about me than the shop. But something (or Someone) inside me urged me to press on.

We had been open four weeks, and there was zero indication that God would provide my release. Yes, I did feel like I was in prison. My older brother, Andy, who was busy enough in law school, generously volunteered to let me train him so he could give me an occasional break. It was on one of these days that he told me to go home for a few hours. "Enjoy the sunshine, go on a walk," Andy said.

Instead, I pulled down all the blinds in my apartment so I *couldn't* see the beautiful day. If I couldn't enjoy it, I didn't want to see it. I found myself on the floor, amidst loads of laundry strewn about. Speaking of laundry, my sweet sister, Rachel, had been doing my laundry for me. I started crying and entertained really bad thoughts of just ending it all.

In my desperation, I somehow made a good decision. I called my mom. I told her I needed her to speak truth over me. As she quoted Scripture and prayed for me, I interrupted her as I sensed an urgency to talk to God myself. I asked her to stay on the phone with me as I did. I felt compelled to surrender. *But hadn't I already done that—multiple times?* I thought. *I guess it can't hurt.* Mom agreed to stay on the phone with me as long as I needed.

"God, if You want me to run this coffee shop for the rest of my life, I will." Maybe that's all God wanted me to say, but I snuck in one last request—as if He didn't already know! "But, God, please, please, please send someone to help!"

At this point, I felt dehydrated from crying, and I sounded like Miss Piggy with all the snot that had accumulated in my nose. My glasses had fallen off, so I couldn't make out what was in front of me. I reached out and snatched the closest piece of laundry and blew my nose into it. As I pulled it away from my face, I noticed it was a pair of underwear! And that right there, is when I knew I had hit rock bottom. I didn't even know if it was clean or dirty, and I didn't care.

I pulled myself off the floor and splashed some water on my face before heading back to Overflow. Once back, I sat down to check our email. Among a myriad of new messages, one jumped out to me. It was titled "Need Help?" *Yes please!* I thought.

A woman named Kate introduced herself as the manager of a coffee shop. She said she was looking for a change and came across our website. That was the first clue that God was involved. We were having major issues with our site. No one could find it. Instead, they'd get images of overflowing toilets!

Kate went on to say that our shop looked beautiful, everything appeared to be going smoothly, and we probably didn't need any help. Clearly, she had not stumbled upon the dozens of ads we had out there basically begging for a manager! She said she was looking for a place to pour her blood, sweat, and tears into. *Ha, fresh body fluids!* I thought. *Mine are spent, so she is just the person for the job! Perfect!*

I wasted no time and contacted Kate immediately. She came over that afternoon and met with my dad and me. It was an instant connection. Kate was kind, warm, competent, and confident. She shared her story about growing discontent and discouraged in her current job, feeling like she was supposed to be somewhere else.

Kate showed great vulnerability when she shared that earlier that afternoon, she was in tears in her truck, crying out to God about her situation, then calling her dad for encouragement. I asked her about what time this occurred, which I'm sure seemed like an odd question. Get this. It was the exact time I was on my floor crying out to God, then calling my mom! Then I asked, "Did you by chance…" I hesitated, "blow your nose into your underwear?" Fortunately for her, that's where our story differed.

Needless to say, we hired Kate on the spot. She started the next day. I was going to stick around for a few weeks to help with her transition, but she basically was ready to run the place within her first hour on the clock. I've never been so happy to get the boot!

Overflow went on to have a great run. It was a very popular spot. We even won an award from the city which was presented by the mayor.

My knight in shining armor did finally come into my life (more about him later!), and he proposed to me outside Overflow by our waterfall and pond. After a few years, my brother, Jeff, took over managing and did a fantastic job. Eventually, it became clear that the right move was to sell the building to developers. Our extended family celebrated Thanksgiving at Overflow in 2016 before closing its doors.

As we enjoyed our Thanksgiving meal in the last year of owning the coffee shop, I had a very sweet memory come to mind. I must tell you about it because it encompasses my biggest takeaway from that whole season of my life: God sees me. Just a few weeks before the opening of Overflow, I was sitting on my bed, literally crying out to God. I passionately told Him how hard it was and how I wished He could come down and give me a hug. It was a quick break at home before I pulled myself together (mostly) and headed back out the door. As I walked down the few steps from the front door to the sidewalk, I passed a mom and her young son, who looked to be about eighteen months old. They were sitting together in the sunshine on the steps. I gave the mom a forced smile and made a beeline for my car. Before I reached my car, I heard the pitter-patter of tiny feet coming up behind me. I turned around to see the sweet little boy toddling after me with his arms stretched high in the air.

He stopped and stared at me with his arms still extended. I looked at him and then his mom. She looked at her son and then at me. Confused, she said, "He's usually really shy. It looks like maybe he wants to give you a hug?" As I bent down and scooped this little boy up, he wrapped his arms around my neck and gave me the best hug of my life. I knew in that moment, proven beyond a shadow of a doubt, that God had not forgotten me. God did answer my desperate prayer that day, as He did many other times. He sent a hug in a tiny, little, adorable package!

Ten years later, I tracked down this little boy and his mom and arranged a time to meet with them. I shared the story with eleven-year-old Seth of how God used him to bring me comfort and care. I gave him a bag of Hershey's Hugs and told him that God has many great plans and purposes for  his life—some of which He fulfilled years ago.

My parents kept their word and paid off my school debt. However, the very best thing I earned from that season was what

I learned. I learned that God is enough. I learned that when He calls, He equips. I learned that just because I am equipped by God, it does not mean the job will be or feel easy. I learned that God has a purpose for pain. God can take a test and make it a testimony, am I right? God can take a mess and turn it into a message. In fact, "Overwhelmed to Overflowing" is one of my most requested talks! God literally turned my mess into a message!

I truly hope my messy message has been meaningful for you. I imagine at some point you've felt overwhelmed, anxious, or perhaps depressed. That's a tough place to be. If that's where you are right now, my heart hurts for you. But I'm also so hopeful for you! Because I have no doubt that God sees you. He hears you. He's with you. Don't be afraid to ask for help. I wish I could give you a hug, but I'm entrusting you into the arms of the biggest and best hugger as I pray Romans 15:13 for you.

God's Word says... "May the God of hope fill you with all joy and peace as you trust in Him, so that you may overflow with hope by the power of the Holy Spirit." (Romans 15:13)

Let's Talk to God...

Lord,

When I get overwhelmed, please remind me to look to You. Forgive me for the times I try to do things in my own strength. Please don't waste any of the trials I've been through and will go through. Use them to grow my character and my faith and draw others to You. *Amen.*

It's Your Turn!

If you are feeling overwhelmed or alone, write down the name of a friend, a pastor, a caring family member, or a professional counselor:

_____

Did you do it? Now put this book down and call them! I mean it. *Now.*

■　■　■

If you are feeling happy and healthy emotionally (yay!), ask God to bring to your mind someone in your life who could use encouragement. Write down their name(s).

_____

_____

_____

Now put a bookmark here (I'll wait for you) and either call them, text them, or show up unannounced with a meal or flowers and a hug. Do it. *Now.*

Chapter 6

Nicknames and Domains

DO YOU HAVE A NICKNAME? Do you like it? I've found they
can go either way. Having been "blessed" (note the sarcasm)
with the last name Barnhart at birth, I am all too familiar with
nicknames gone wrong. In middle school, I was called Molly
Barnyard, Molly Barndoor, and my favorite—Molly Barnfart. My
brother, Andy, acquired that name first since he had a reputation
of having bad gas. I would often see him sitting outside his class-
room, exiled to the hallway at our high school because his teacher
and classmates couldn't handle the smell. (Sorry, Andy. Enough
about that.)

It was sometime in my teen years that I decided I wanted to
be called M.J. for my name, Molly Jean. It was only coincidental that those were also the initials of Michael Jordan, Michael
Jackson, and Spiderman's girlfriend. I learned pretty quickly that
nicknames are *given by others*, and all my attempts to get my
friends to call me M.J. were futile. There was a fleeting moment

of hope, however, when my cousin, Danny, called me M.J. I must have acted a little too excited because he never called me by that name again.

When I went to college, I figured that would be the perfect time to make a switch. Volleyball practices began before classes started in the fall, so I determined to introduce myself as M.J. to my new teammates. As each girl went around the circle introducing themselves, I grew more and more excited to debut my new name. *Just one more girl to go, then it's my turn,* I thought as I was daydreaming about my new identity. I was rudely awakened from my dream when I heard the girl next to me introduce herself. "Hi, my name is Mary Jo, but everyone calls me M.J." *What?! How can this be happening?! Can't we just call her Mary Jo and I'll be M.J.?* Turns out she'd been called that all her life, so I continued on as Molly. The *real* M.J. and I became friends.

Fast forward a couple years. I was out of college, had developed and designed the family coffee shop, and was speaking full time. Oh—and I did have my other newly acquired nickname— Cheese Ball Chick! Little did I know that as I was busy speaking to teens and handing out cheese balls, my future husband was doing a little research on me.

A friend of ours, who I had lost touch with, sent him a text one night and told him to go to MollyBarnhart.com, the website domain I used for speaking. Apparently, she felt we'd make a really good match but didn't happen to tell me about it! My future hubby, let's call him Craig because that's his name, clicked on my site and "met me" for the first time. Some people call that stalking—just saying.

Craig clicked around to learn about the coffee shop I developed, saw some video clips of me speaking to teens, and learned that I bring joy to the world one cheese ball at a time. He was intrigued enough to continue stalking—I mean researching—me and clicked on a little tab titled "Fun Stuff." Maybe he shouldn't have, because this tab took him to a page with nearly twenty ridiculous videos of me doing obnoxious things like dancing around my apartment while wearing a wig with a stuffed monkey in my footy pajamas to look pregnant while lip synching to a Disney soundtrack. I cringe even now thinking that was his first impression of me. He still cringes too, ha!

There is an explanation to that video (and the others!). My friend Melanie was overdue with her first pregnancy, so I thought creating a labor-inducing video while I was snowed in at my apartment was a good idea. She thought it was funny and suggested I put it on my website to show teens they can have a ton of fun in life—all natural. Contrary to most people's opinion, there were no drugs or alcohol involved in the filming of that video.

Craig claims he saw enough and thought I might be just a bit too crazy for him. But then seemingly out of nowhere, he started to hear my name mentioned in different circles. We lived two hours apart, so this was a bit unusual.

Craig must not have been *completely* turned off by me because he paid not one, but two visits to...guess where...Overflow, the coffee shop I had designed and opened! You might be thinking, what's the big deal about that? Remember, he lived two hours away. And he doesn't even drink coffee! Now that is truly stalking. I didn't happen to be there either time, so he was able to remain undetected.

Shortly after his second trip to the coffee shop, Craig went to a planning meeting for an upcoming youth event. While discussing who to book as their speaker, my name came up *again*. Craig had flashbacks to the images of me in the wig and footy pajamas and tried to remain calm. "Craig, do you know Molly Barnhart?" someone asked.

He probably stumbled over his words and said something like "Um, no. Never met her, and I haven't stalked her at the coffee shop or creeped on her website either."

Craig was relieved when his lifelong friend, Heather, another youth pastor, interrupted him and said she was going to be getting together with me in a few weeks. Her good friend, Roxy, was a health teacher at a local school I spoke at. Roxy wanted to introduce me to Heather since she was a speaker too and had years more experience that I could glean from. At the end of the meeting, Craig pulled Heather aside and admitted he *did* know about me and had been to my website. She agreed to go "undercover" and do some recon work to see what I was all about. "But don't mention my name!" he insisted.

A few weeks later, and having no idea I was being researched, I met Heather and Roxy for lunch. We had an instant connection and great conversation. Heather asked me what I envisioned for my future. I told the ladies I felt God's confirmation to continue speaking but how I would love to someday marry and partner with a husband in ministry. "It would be awesome if he was a speaker too, maybe a youth pastor," I told them. I had no idea that I was describing Heather's good friend, Craig, and that she was "sent" to scope me out.

I also had no idea that I had already won Heather's approval. I'm sure the cheese balls helped. Now that I know the back story, the funny look on Heather's face and the steam coming out of her nostrils and ears makes total sense. She had promised Craig she would not bring up his name, so she sat silently, which is not like Heather, and wished the matchmaking could begin.

Roxy, having no idea about this secret investigation, blurted out, "Hey Heather, what about your friend, Craig Sanborn?" Heather took a deep breath and started sharing as if it was the first time it crossed her mind. Roxy only knew about Craig because he had spoken at her health class one time five years prior, but she knew enough about him to think we could be a potential pair.

Both ladies talked over each other as they excitedly described this "great guy." I picked up words like youth pastor, loves teens, athletic, good looking, loves Jesus, has integrity, great character, fun, funny, speaker...I think the whole restaurant wanted to meet this guy. I know I did!

Heather didn't stop there. She called Craig! She didn't let on that he already knew me, but she teased him by saying "Hey Craig, I'm out to eat with Roxy—remember her? And oh, this gal named Molly Barnhart. Have you ever heard of her?" Craig was on the other end shaking his head and rolling his eyes.

Our dinner concluded with Heather promising Craig would call me. I was a little confused how she could be so confident, but I took her word and anxiously awaited his call. A few days went by, and I heard nothing. A week passed. Still nothing. I decided to take matters into my own hands and get a hold of him myself. While I am a go-getter, I also am old-fashioned when it comes to dating, so making the first move was out of character for me.

Okay, okay, I admit. I did a little stalking of my own. I went to CraigSanborn.org, his speaking website at the time, immediately after meeting with the ladies. After seven long days of waiting for Craig to write or call, I hesitantly filled out the contact form saying something casual like, "Hey Craig, supposedly we have a mutual friend. Just thought I'd say hello." I wasn't going to ask him out on a date. I just wanted to help things along. The moment I hit "submit," I totally regretted it. I had just long enough to slap my forehead and scold myself before a message popped up. "Message failed to send." "Thank you, Jesus!" I yelled.

I decided to be patient (not an easy thing for me) and keep waiting. Another week went by, and just as I was about to give up on this Craig Sanborn guy, I received an email with a subject line, "Take Two" from guess who!

CRAIG SANBORN!

He introduced himself and shared that Heather suggested we get in touch. He told me this was his second attempt at reaching me because he had sent a message via my website nearly two weeks earlier. When he didn't hear back, he got my email from Heather. He went on to ask me out on a date to which I said YES!

As to my website, I discovered that there was a very short window when my contact form was not delivering my messages. However, it didn't give the sender a nice message like Craig's site gave me, so Craig assumed I received the message. I'm so glad Craig persevered and didn't give up. What a guy!

We met a few weeks later for our first date. Since I needed to host a karaoke event at the coffee shop later that night, we decided to meet in the parking lot of Overflow. When I asked if he needed directions to the coffee shop, he replied with, "I'll figure it out." Ha! That's because he had already been there twice stalking me! Remember?! I recall seeing him as I got out of my car. *Wow. He is way better looking in person!* I thought. That mock turtle-neck and half a smile I saw on his website didn't do him justice.

Just as I was closing my car door, I noticed my cheese balls in the back. I hesitated and heard a still small voice say, "You've got to be yourself." So I strapped them on and went to meet my future husband. My very first words to him were, "Hey, do you want a cheese ball?" He indulged and the rest is history.

Wait, hold on. There's another incredible part to this story! We got in Craig's car (He opened my door! What a gentleman!) and drove to an incredibly romantic restaurant— Applebee's. It was so easy to talk, and I found myself falling for him very quickly.

My giddiness only grew when he offered to pray for our dinner.

During dinner, he told me that he had a dream about me. *Okay* ...I thought. This might be getting weird. He went on to tell me how he had been to my website and seen all the crazy videos. My face went from pale to pink to bright red! I couldn't even remember all the videos I had posted, but I could remember enough to be totally embarrassed. He told me that just the night before, he dreamt that while he was praying for our meal, I was secretly video recording him from under the table!

We both laughed, and I assured him I had not recorded his prayer, but inside, I was mortified. *He must think I'm totally nuts!* First, he sees all those stupid videos, then I wear cheese balls on our first date! Who does that?! Someone who doesn't want to be asked out for a second date, that's who does that!

As we drove back to the coffee shop, I focused on acting as normal as humanly possible. I had to get ready to host the karaoke party, and he had a two-hour drive back home, so we said goodbye. I was anxiously awaiting a "Let's do this again." or "Hey, are you free next week?" Nope.

Craig was very sweet and kind and said he had a great time ...but he didn't say he wanted to see me again. Bummer. Later that night, after the event, I went out for some late-night appetizers with friends. They all asked how the date went, and I told them exactly how I felt. "I'm very interested in him. He seems like a great guy, but I'm pretty sure he thinks I'm crazy because he didn't even hint at another date." My friends consoled me and went on with their evening, but I couldn't get Craig out of my mind. So right there, in the Perkins booth, I offered a silent plea of a prayer up to God.

Lord, I really like this guy. Could You somehow let him know that I'm not crazy? Well, that might be a lie. Umm...maybe just put in a good word for me. And if there is any way that he is interested in me, would You please nudge him to let me know sooner than later? Thanks and Amen.

I got back to my apartment after 1 a.m. that night. Before jumping in bed, I quickly checked Facebook. I saw the little icon that told me I had a message. It was from...

Guess who.

Yup!

CRAIG SANBORN!

He told me that he had a great time on our date and that as he drove home, he had a lot of time to think. "It occurred to me that you might think that I think you are crazy."

I'm not kidding! That is exactly what he wrote! "So am I crazy?" I yelled at the computer. He went on, "I want you to know that I get it, I like it, and I'm wondering if I could see you again."

"Ahhhhhhhhhhhhhhhh!!!!!!!!!!! He doesn't think I'm crazy!" I yelled again. My poor roommate disagreed as she woke up dazed and confused. Actually, as I reread his message (about 100 times), I realized he never actually said I *wasn't* crazy. He just said he liked it. That was okay with me.

Craig went on to invite me to join his youth group at a Minnesota Twins baseball game and roller skating the very next day! I wasn't able to make the game, but I joined them for skating. My cheese balls helped me make a good impression on his youth group kids, which helped me gain their approval—which of course was very important to Craig. Seeing him in youth pastor mode only made me like him more.

I guess his fondness of me was growing too, because later that night I got another message from him. This time he wrote:

"Brace yourself. I have a really important question to ask you." *Umm ...is he going to propose!? I like him, but that's moving kinda quick!* I thought. "What is your middle name?" He asked. *Phew!* I breathed a sigh of relief. This is an easy answer.

"I hope your middle name is Jo," he continued. *Wait, what?!* I thought.

I wrote back, "Sorry to disappoint you, but my middle name is not Jo. It's Jean. I hope that's okay with you."

I just about fell out of my chair when I read his response. "Oh, that's perfect! I just want to be able to call you M.J."

I pinched myself to make sure I wasn't dreaming. *That's the nickname I've wanted to be called all my life!* Now I was officially ready for him to propose! *Maybe I should just ask HIM!* I pondered for about half a second before I slapped my forehead again and came back to reality. Things only got better from there. Our second date led to a third and fourth and so on. I'm skipping a TON of great parts, because honestly, we'll probably just write a book about our love story someday!

But I can't resist—I *have* to tell you this part! About two months after we met, it occurred to me that if I married Craig, I'd become Molly Sanborn. Then I would need to ditch my domain, MollyBarnhart.com, and get one with my new name. Now I know you are thinking that I jumped online to buy that domain right then—no, no, I'm not that crazy. I just needed to take a peek and see if it was even available.

So I typed in www.mollysanborn.com and a screen popped up that said, "This domain is taken." But there wasn't actually a website, so I had hope that whoever owned it might be willing to sell it to me in the future. So ...I did a little digging. I had recently learned how to find out who owns domains, so I went to the site, typed in my potential future name, and guess what popped up under who it was registered to.

Seriously.

Guess.

CRAIG SANBORN! (You are getting good at this guessing game!) And then it listed his complete address and phone number, so I *knew* it was him! I started hyperventilating, running in place, and flapping my arms like a chicken. I ran into my roommate's room and screamed at her. "I feel like I just got engaged!" I yelled. "But he hasn't even asked me yet!" My roommate shared in my excitement, and I started planning my wedding. Well, okay, not quite yet, but I was certain it was going to happen.

I didn't know if I should say anything to Craig about my discovery or not, so I just waited. I thought maybe I wasn't supposed to find it, and he was going to use it as part of a proposal or something.

He did propose a few months later by washing my feet and asking if he could serve me like Jesus came to serve. I screamed, "Yes!" Then I finally confessed that I knew about the website and totally freaked out (in a good way). He smiled and said "Great. That played out exactly like I hoped it would."

Years later, no one calls me M.J. but Craig. And I think that's pretty special. Well, I should say, there is the guy at Costco who does, and I was really confused for a while until I realized my membership card says M.J. Sanborn!

I can't help but think that just as Craig looked forward to me discovering the website, God looked forward to my reaction of hearing Craig call me M.J. for the first time. I am pretty sure God was giddy with me—probably not doing the chicken dance, but I definitely think He was joining me in my joy.

Maybe you're wondering what God has to do with nicknames. Everything!

As I invested in my relationship with God as a teenager, spent time with Him, journaled, talked to Him about my crushes, my hopes, my dreams, my disappointments, and prayed for my future husband, I was "delighting" in God. And as I did, I believe the Lord was putting desires in my heart that He was excited to fulfill one day.

I don't think it's too far-fetched to think that God put the idea of calling me M.J. in Craig's mind. Do *you* think it's just coincidence? It could be I suppose, but I'm going to go with God, because the rest of the Bible tells a story about a God who is intimately involved in the lives of those who let Him in.

God's Word says..."Delight yourself in the Lord, and He will give you the desires of your heart." (Psalm 37:4)

Let's Talk to God...

Dear Lord,

Help me delight in You, Your ways, and Your Word. Thank You for the promise that as I do, You will instill and fulfill the desires of my heart. *Amen.*

It's Your Turn!

Do you know what your name means? Do a quick online search (Don't forget your middle name!). Write down what you find:

While you're at it, do a little research on what some of God's names mean:

El Shaddai:

Jehovah Nissi:

Jehovah Raah:

Jehovah Rapha:

Jehovah Shammah:

Jehovah Tsidkenu:

El Olam:

Jehovah Jireh:

Jehovah Shalom:

Which one do you need to remind yourself about right now?

Chapter 7

A Sinking Feeling

THE RAIN CLOUDS WERE OMINOUS, and the temperature
was dropping, but that wasn't going to stop us from enjoying
some time on a lake in northern Minnesota. My two brothers,
Andy and Jeff, my husband, Craig, and I were spending Memorial Day weekend at my parents' cabin, and we were determined to
fish—rain or shine.

We layered just about every article of clothing we had to
ensure we'd be warm. We even rigged up custom rain gear out of
plastic garbage bags and duct tape. We looked like a homemade
version of the Ghostbusters.

After a thirty-minute drive down a gravel road, we reached
the remote lake and were thrilled to have it all to ourselves. More
fish for us! We situated ourselves in Andy's small aluminum boat.
Jeff snagged the best seat in the house—a swivel office chair Andy
had bolted to the bow. Craig and I sat on benches in the middle
as Andy manned his brand-new trolling motor at the rear.

We wasted no time casting our lines into the water. The fish were nibbling, but we decided to kick up the motor to find a better spot farther away from shore. Little did we know that our bobbers would soon have company. Because of a weight imbalance we were totally unaware of, our boat went from a floating watercraft to a submarine—literally. The boat took a nosedive. The frigid water rushed over our feet, and within seconds, the entire boat was under water. We experienced a sinking feeling—literally and figuratively!

We found ourselves struggling to catch our breath and stay afloat in the icy cold water. Our thick clothing and plastic bags quickly took on water and began to weigh us down. As the reality of our situation sank in, we became desperate to locate the life jackets, which we assumed would pop up at any moment.

"Andy, where are the life jackets?" we questioned. No words were necessary. If Andy was a dog, his tail would have been between his legs as he gave the guiltiest look of shame and regret

I have ever seen. In his excitement and exuberance to get on the water, he had forgotten the life jackets in the trunk of the car. Too bad I didn't bring my cheese balls in the boat. It would have been a flotation device and food all in one.

With no life jackets, our only hope was to cling to the side of the overturned boat. We decided to work together and pull the boat to shore, which was over a football field away. Sensing we were making no progress, I felt like my energy would be better used swimming to land to go for help. Craig and my brothers pleaded with me to ditch the layers of clothes I was wearing, but I felt confident I could make it in a winter jacket, leather gloves, a hat, three shirts, two pairs of pants, two pairs of socks, and tennis shoes—not to mention the two bags around my feet and the two huge garbage bags wrapped around each leg. After all, I used to be a lifeguard at Village Creek Bible Camp. *I was made for this moment*, I thought.

I'll never forget when I had the realization that I was drowning. I liked my shoes and jeans a little too much to let them fall to the bottom of the lake. Now those very things I clung to so tightly were pulling me under.

The boys and the boat were now too far from me to hear my whimpers. That's all I could let out of my labored lungs. It was then I remembered what I had learned in my lifeguard training—most drowning victims are silent. Fortunately, my pitiful pleas were heard by God.

By what can only be described as a divine intervention, I survived (obviously, since I'm telling you this story)! God must have sent a boat load of angels (sorry for the pun) to drag me in, because by this time I had taken on double my weight in water and looked like an Oompa Loompa. After being escorted to shore, I lay there like a beached whale.

Meanwhile back at the boat, the boys finally realized why they weren't making any progress. Unbeknownst to them, the anchor had fallen to the bottom of the lake and was preventing them from going anywhere. They were hopelessly and needlessly exhausting themselves by pulling on an anchored vessel.

Jeff was next to abandon the boat and swim to shore, but not before climbing atop the overturned boat where he stripped down to his boxers and safely encased his wallet and car keys in his bundle of clothes which he held above his head during his swim. He made it to shore much more quickly than I had, and he didn't require heavenly intervention.

I wasn't anywhere near ready to pull myself up off my face, but Jeff reminded me why I swam to shore in the first place—to go get HELP. He and I took off in the direction we *thought* would take us to the boat launch. There were no trails in this thickly wooded area, so we blazed our own. Picture this. I am *still* wearing everything I started with, and Jeff is *only* wearing underwear.

Jeff set a grueling pace as he ran like Forrest Gump, stopping for nothing. He shoved branches out of his way, which whipped back just in time to whack me over and over again. I felt like I was back in a middle school game of dodgeball.

The only reason I could keep up with Jeff was because I was convinced that I was being chased by a bear. Since I was still wearing garbage bags (I didn't want to litter), I was a great target for a bear, I thought, since I know they scrounge in trash bins. My only consolation was the realization that a bear might give up on me since I had so many layers to get through. My nearly naked brother would be a much better choice.

We outran all the bears that were in my imagination and made it back to the boat launch. Unfortunately, there were no humans in sight, but maybe that was a good thing since we emerged from the woods looking like Swamp Thing 1 and Swamp Thing 2.

Back at the boat, Craig was the last one standing, rather sitting. He was perched on top of the overturned boat, calling for help. Andy opted to swim to shore, but not before dropping his shoes and pants to the bottom of the lake.

After thirty minutes of shivering and shouting atop the boat, Craig was relieved to see a pontoon appear off in the distance. It felt like an eternity until the rescuers reached him. After assessing the situation, they decided to retrieve Andy on shore, then come back for Craig and the boat.

I wonder what thoughts went through their heads as they approached Andy who was not only without clothes but also missing his front tooth! Yes, you read that correctly–Andy's tooth was missing. It hadn't come out when the boat went down, but Andy had actually taken it out and put it in his tackle box just moments before we submarined. My brother lost his two front teeth in an accident years ago, and had them replaced with fake teeth, one of which had recently become loose. Completely clueless that we were just minutes from going under, Andy had placed his loose tooth in the tackle box to keep it safe, because to replace it would cost over $600. Now his tooth and tackle box were either lodged under the boat (he hoped!) or sitting on the bottom of the lake.

Craig, still fully dressed in his nearly frozen clothes, was eager to jump to a more stable watercraft. He held a rope attached to the upside-down boat as the pontoon dragged it back to where we first launched.

If the pontooners (I'm going to say that's a word) weren't already convinced we were an odd bunch of hillbillies, that was solidified when they saw Jeff and I whooping and hollering at the boat launch. Since the boat arrived bottom up, we had to get *back* in the water to flip it upright. This was no small task.

Once that mission was accomplished, our next goal was to locate all the goods—particularly Andy's tooth. We scoured the boat and surrounding water for the tackle box, but it was nowhere to be found. Andy's tooth wasn't the only thing that sank. Our hearts did as we realized his brand-new battery for the trolling motor was also missing, along with some very expensive fishing poles he had borrowed from a friend.

With no spare clothes in the car and only one pair of big rubber waders, my brothers opted to stay in their underwear, with Craig following suit—not in his birthday suit—but almost! I made a fashion statement in the oversized overalls and couldn't decide if I preferred feeling soggy in my wet clothes or sticky in the rubbery waders.

The heat was on full blast as we drove back to the cabin. We huddled around the wood burning stove at the cabin warming our rumps and other extremities. As we watched our fingers and toes slowly turn from white to pink, we discussed our plan for the following day.

We were determined to recover our lost goods—especially Andy's tooth. We had already suffered a significant financial blow since cell phones and my brand-new camera were ruined due to water damage. Bye-bye BlackBerry phone. Bye-bye camera which held the only proof of this experience. Had the camera been working, we could have captured the next saga in photo and video, and that honestly might be the only way you would believe what happened the next day.

Andy, Jeff, and I committed to the rescue mission, and Craig committed to stay back and "pray," which may have included a nap. But before resting his eyes, he rolled them a time or two as he witnessed our sibling shenanigans. Andy led the circus—I mean charge—with a brief tutorial on the creative contraptions he had brainstormed for our mission.

He dictated his ideas with passion and urgency as he cast a vision for our venture. I have to be honest though—it was a little hard taking him seriously with his lisp. "In order to find our lotht itemths," he shared, "we need to uthe a hothe for an underwater breathing apparatith."

So we set to it. We grabbed a fifteen-foot garden hothe, I mean hose, which Andy intended to use as his breathing tube. It was hard to keep a straight face when he said, "We need to be able to thee underwater, tho we mutht find a pair of goggleths."

We drove to a nearby vacation lodge in hopes of borrowing some goggles. I still laugh as I remember Andy explaining our calamity to the front desk staff at Lutsen Resort. He promised them he was good for it, but had no money, credit card, or ID to give in exchange since they were all in his wallet at the bottom of the lake. In normal circumstances, he could just flash his charming smile, but that would do more damage than good in this situation.

They must have felt for us, because we got the goggles and hit the road, but not before asking God for favor and direction in our quest. We continued to pray while en route—specifically that we would find Andy's tackle box *securely shut* with the tooth safe inside. Even though Andy remembered latching it, we wondered if it had been knocked open in all the chaos. By this time, his tooth could have been in the belly of a fish!

Once at the lake, we put on our wet suits and securely stowed the life jackets in the boat, two things that would have proved very helpful the day before. As we trolled into the lake, we let down a yard rake whose handle we extended with a broom handle and duct tape. We combed the bottom of the lake with this flimsy redneck contraption, hoping to snag one of the fishing poles.

Believe it or not—it actually worked! Catching a fishing pole bolstered our confidence and made the boys eager to enter the water. They were convinced we had found the spot where we went down, but I had a sinking feeling they were wrong.

My confidence rested on the image ingrained in my mind from the day before when I was swimming for my life: the branches of a birch tree extending into the water as though they were reaching out to me. Those branches had become my finish line, and now, not even twenty-four hours later, they had become my reference point. But we were nowhere near the birch tree. Though I adamantly explained my reasoning to my stubborn brothers, they disregarded my suggestion and insisted on searching the area where the pole had been found.

I'll never forget Andy attempting to use the garden hose as an extended snorkel. He entered the frigid water, only slightly more bearable because of the wet suit, and we handed him one end of the hose. Jeff and I were tasked with the job of holding the other end of the hose upright in order to supply oxygen.

Andy wrapped his lips around the end of the hose and disappeared into the dark water. We heard some muffled noises, and not long after, he emerged from the water looking a bit blue and sounding quite winded. This only confirmed Jeff's and my suspicions, that this system would not work.

We tried to talk Andy out of this nonsense, but he wasn't ready to give up. He tried a few more times, and finally relented after Jeff nearly drowned him. Andy was trying to breath air through the hose while Jeff accidentally let the other end of the hose fall into the water on the far side of the boat. We heard some gurgling followed by a very irritated Andy coming up for air!

Not only did the underwater breathing system not work, seeing through the muck while down there was impossible. The water was still so cold that the capacity to hold one's breath was cut in half. The boys discovered that diving from the boat was the only way to get to the bottom fast enough to still have some air left in their lungs. They would rely on their hands to feel along the bottom.

They took turns getting in and out of the boat and diving to the bottom. Each time they would enter and exit the boat, it rocked so much we nearly capsized. I had flashbacks to the day before and quickly put on a life jacket. Notice, I did not do any of the diving. Not because I was unwilling to help, but because I was still certain we were searching in the wrong place!

After over an hour draining themselves with dives from the boat and blind searches through the muck twelve feet below, they finally agreed to pull up anchor and head to the area in line with the birch tree. Skeptical of the new spot and utterly exhausted, they dug deep and prepared for what could be another hour of diving. While I was pretty certain we were in the general area, there was really no way of knowing the exact spot. I prayed fervently that God would direct their dives and the sweeping motions of their hands. Jeff and I waited anxiously as Andy took his first blind dive down in the new spot.

It was only seconds, but it felt like minutes. Andy's fist surfaced first, triumphantly holding our blue bag of mini M&M's we had been snacking on the day before! His other hand grasped the ultimate prize—the tackle box—still shut tight! Inside, safe and sound, was his tooth! We also recovered the battery and Andy's wallet with all its contents.

Our celebration echoed over the waters. My brothers apologized for not listening to me sooner, and we all praised and thanked God for His provision and protection.

We nicknamed Andy "Tooth 'n Tackle" and thanked God for that birch tree which had become a very precious point of reference.

As I reflect on our adventures, I can't help but think of dozens of spiritual illustrations and Scriptures that relate to this story. Here's just one.

My foolish refusal to let go of what was hindering me nearly cost me my life. I was aware of what was holding me back, but sometimes it's not as obvious—like the guys trying to move an anchored boat. What I needed to do was to exchange my weighty, water-logged clothes for a life jacket. In spiritual terms, we need to exchange our sin for a Savior. I've heard people compare Jesus to a life jacket, and until my bout with the boat, it never really sunk in. But now it's an analogy I can relate to!

On Memorial Day weekend 2011, I called out to God to save my life. Years earlier, as a young girl, I called on the name of Jesus to save my soul. I had become aware that my sins separated me from God and destined me for an eternity apart from Him. I simply did what Romans 10:9 says. I confessed with my mouth that Jesus is Lord, and I believed in my heart that God raised Him from the dead. And I was saved.

If only getting saved on the water was that simple! Oh yeah —I suppose it could have been. If we had only remembered the life jackets—and put them ON!

God's Word says..."Therefore, since we are surrounded by such a huge crowd of witnesses to the life of faith, let us strip off every weight that slows us down, especially the sin that so easily trips us up." (Hebrews 12:1 NLT)

Let's Talk to God...

Dear Lord,

Please reveal to me the things that are weighing me down. Enable me with Your strength to throw them off and keep them off. And please help me fix my eyes on You always—especially in troubling times. And whether for the first time or as a declaration of what I already have believed: Jesus, You are Lord. Thank You for saving me. *Amen.*

It's Your Turn!

Did you pray that prayer? No worries if you're not ready for that. But if you asked God to reveal things that are weighing you down, I believe He will!

Take some time to allow God to bring to your mind anything He might be asking you to let go of. Would you be willing to write it down below and drop it to the bottom of the metaphorical lake?

Chapter 8

Open Heart Surgery?!

MY CAT WILL BE FOREVER TERRIFIED of pregnancy tests. No, no, no, I didn't *give* my cat a pregnancy test (that'd be weird), but I did chase her while wildly waving one around, yelling, "I'm pregnant! I'm pregnant!" (That's not weird at all.) She was the only one in the house when I saw that teensy-weensy plus sign appear, and since I *had* to celebrate with someone, I picked her.

She was relieved when Craig came home and my exuberant excitement (can you say those two words together?) was directed toward him instead. One of the first things I did was make an appointment at our local clinic. I wanted confirmation ASAP! They weren't on my timetable and scheduled an appointment for me to come in two long weeks later. At least that gave me time to come up with my "birthing plan." I was an over-zealous, first-time mom—yes, I know, for those of you rolling your eyes.

Boy, are there a lot of birthing plan details and options to consider! Birthing stools, birthing beds, birthing tubs, epidural, all natural, C-Section, playlists, midwives, doctors, doulas (what's that?), husbands, at home, at the hospital, in the car if you don't make it in time, and the list goes on. Being an athlete and an optimist, I decided that going all natural (no drugs for pain relief) was the superior choice. I figured I needed some coaching, so I scheduled an appointment to meet with a midwife right after my first ultrasound.

Finally, the day arrived to see our baby for the first time. The technician smeared some cold jelly on my belly and used what looked like a wand (more professionally known as a transducer) to locate and look at our baby. He did some measuring, clicked on his keyboard about a hundred times, and snapped some images. Then he let us hear the teeny-tiny, super-fast heartbeat. Wow. Just wow.

As Craig and I were teary eyed and awestruck, the technician continued to prod my belly. Then he started to say "Hmmm…." and "Oh, my…" and "What's that?" and "I don't think that's supposed to be there."

Uh oh. I thought. *He must see the box of Thin Mint Girl Scout cookies I just ate to curb my pregnancy cravings. How embarrassing.* I wish that's what he was concerned about, but his continued unprofessional outbursts coupled with his facial expressions confirmed our fears. Something was wrong. I didn't know it then, but it is a rule of thumb that sonographers do not give medical advice or a diagnosis, but he must have missed that day of class.

He went on to tell us that it would appear I had a very large cyst, larger than any he had ever seen, and it was likely going to grow and could impact the development of our baby. He told us to schedule an appointment as soon as possible at a bigger hospital that was one hour away.

Then he tossed a towel at me so I could wipe off the goop. As soon as he left, I used it instead to wipe my eyes which had been holding back a load of tears. Craig prayed over the baby and me. I'm sure he said something encouraging though I couldn't focus.

I wasn't really in the mood to meet the midwife now, but we kept our appointment. It turned out to be a good distraction as we toured the birthing suites. *Birthing suites? Wow, that sounds fancy!* I thought. And they were! The rooms, recently finished, felt like an upscale hotel, yet homey at the same time. "What's that?" Craig asked as he pointed at the birthing tub. "Oh, that's where I could have our baby." I replied. Looking totally confused and slightly concerned, he said, "Shouldn't our baby have swimming lessons first?"

The midwife explained the process of using tubs for birthing, adding that Craig was welcome in the tub too. At this point, Craig had heard enough and suggested he was most comfortable with him relaxing in the tub while I gave birth to our baby in the bed.

Right when we got home, I called the hospital to make an appointment. "As soon as possible," I politely requested. They must not have felt it was nearly as urgent as I did, because they gave me a date that was three weeks away! *Argh! More waiting!* At least that gave me plenty of time to do a little research of my own, thanks to Google. I take that back. NO thanks to Google! Cancer, miscarriage, rupture, surgery, and internal bleeding all came up in my search about cysts.

I finally had the wisdom to x out of all the web pages and open up my email. There I composed a message to my close friends and family, doing what I should have done in the first place. I asked for prayer. I told them I was scared. I told them I was anxious. In return, I received a dozen hope-filled messages that shifted the focus from my fears to my faith in a God who hears me.

When we got to our appointment twenty-one days later (who's counting?), there was yet another opportunity for patience as I was asked to fill out about 1,700 pages of paperwork. OK, maybe it was just seven, but there were A LOT of questions. I eventually got in a rhythm and just started checking "No" all the way down the long list. But then I paused and pondered on the question about heart conditions. This one stumped me, because as a child I had some kind of "mild heart condition," but that felt like a lifetime ago. I felt great and hadn't been to my cardiologist in over ten years.

As a small child, I was diagnosed with aortic stenosis which is basically the narrowing of the aortic valve. A normal person's aortic valve has three flaps or cusps, commonly called a "tricuspid valve," that open and close in sync to allow blood to be pumped out of the heart and into the body. I fall in the 1-2 percent of "abnormal" people (surprise! surprise!) and have only two cusps, called a "bicuspid valve," which can cause the valve to be narrower or stenotic. I was checked yearly as a child and teen with electrocardiograms (EKGs) and echocardiograms to ensure my condition wasn't progressing as I grew up.

One time when I was about eight years old, I blacked out while doing the dishes. My parents, of course, were concerned, but I think it was probably my subconscious way of getting out of doing chores. They took me to my cardiologist who set me up with a heart monitor for three days. They stuck about ten super sticky patches with little sensors, each attached to a wire all around my chest and even on my neck. The uncomfortable cords were attached to a device about the size of an old-school Walkman that I clipped to my pants. It was in the heat of the summer, and I was not allowed to get wet. I couldn't care less about missing a bath, but it was torture not to swim.

To make matters worse, on one of the hottest days, when my siblings were free to swim and play at the local pool, my mom told me to ride my bike to speech therapy. Um, yeah. That's a little-known detail about my life. Thanks to my older brother Andy's influence, I did not learn how to properly say my "r's." *Park* was "pok" and *car* was "cah," for example.

So there I was, riding my banana seat bike with sparkly blue streamers flying in the wind, hot, sweaty, and incredibly itchy from the electronic patches on my body. I was already down in the dumps when a biker gang of tweens came up from behind me. They were teasing and taunting me (probably jealous of my vintage bicycle). "C'mon slow poke! Can't you go any faster?"

I was desperately hoping they wouldn't see any wires pop out from under my tank top. With my embarrassing bike, poofy hair, crooked teeth, poor speech, and scrawny legs, there was not a lack of material for teasing. Just as I thought they were taking off, one of the boys rubbed his front tire against my back tire nearly toppling me to the pavement below. I regained my balance and held back the tears until the bullies disappeared in the distance.

I was relieved when the patches came off a few days later, but I was disappointed to hear that I was not restricted from doing dishes. Turns out my heart could handle that and everything else I did on a daily basis. The blackout must have been from skipping breakfast or locking my knees.

A few years later in middle school there was another scare. During an intense and fast-paced basketball game, in which I played all four quarters, my parents noticed my face go from red to blue to ghostly white. I've always been patriotic that way. I nearly fainted in the locker room, so that meant another trip to the cardiologist. This time they skipped the heart monitor (yes!) and gave me a stress test instead (no!). They put me on a treadmill and slowly increased the speed and incline until I was basically running up Mount Everest at 60 mph. I was running in a hospital gown while connected to a machine via more patches and wires. My heart and I survived the marathon, and I was cleared to continue sports (and chores) with no restrictions.

Sporadic heart scares continued. There was the time in my early twenties when I was getting a haircut at a beauty training school. I was a college student on a budget and looked for any way to save a dime. My hair was pretty long, and the trainee struggled to give me an even trim as my hair fell over the back of the chair. She asked if I minded standing up for my haircut.

I agreed and stood patiently for nearly thirty minutes. *This is the last time I skimp on haircuts,* I thought to myself as my back ached and I started feeling a little woozy. I asked if I could take a break and sit for a minute. The last thing I remember seeing is the garbage can, as I apparently fell to the ground.

I woke up with a bunch of terrified beauty school pupils staring down at me. They had already called 911 and the ambulance was on its way. "I think I'm fine," I insisted. In my rush to get to the appointment on time, I had skipped breakfast. That, with the combination of standing still (knees probably locked *again*), had to be the reason I fainted. Still, they weren't comfortable releasing me without medical attention.

When the paramedics arrived and found out I had a heart condition, they felt it best to take me to the hospital. I was in good spirits the whole time, making friends and cracking jokes with a wet head and half a haircut. After a series of tests, they released me free and clear of any complications having to do with my heart.

Then I called the beauty school back. "Hello, I'm the girl who fainted this morning during my haircut. I was wondering if I could come back and get it finished."

"Ummm…. Hang on a second please," she said on the other end. After about a minute, she came back on the phone, "I'm sorry, but we don't feel comfortable cutting your hair."

Excuse me! I thought. *You don't feel comfortable??? I was the one who was uncomfortable as I stood at attention for a half hour just to get a little trim!*

After waking up on the beauty school floor, taking a ride in an ambulance, and getting an array of tests, it wasn't until this moment that I broke down. Even after crying on the phone and asking them to reconsider, they didn't budge. I'm pretty sure a whole batch of students quit that day, and they couldn't afford to lose any more.

Thankfully, I found a place that *would* finish my haircut and allow me to sit at the same time! Unfortunately, they still charged me full price for half a haircut, but at least I didn't lean to one side anymore.

So, as you can see—I had three pretty significant incidents, but none of them were believed to be a result of my heart. As I sat there in the waiting room, checking "No" to all the questions, I wasn't sure if I should even mention my "mild heart condition."

Well, as you will soon find out, it was a *very* good thing that I did.

I finally got called in for the ultrasound, and fortunately, this sonographer was much more professional and personable. Dr. Pinkerton followed suit. She also happened to be much more informed and quickly set us at ease explaining that the cyst was not uncommon, and it would most likely go away on its own. In fact, it was already smaller than five weeks earlier, and she confirmed that baby was growing strong and healthy. *Phew! And thank You, Jesus!*

Before we wrapped up the appointment, she went over my paperwork, specifically asking me about my history with the aortic stenosis. I gave her a brief run down and told her I hadn't been to the cardiologist in almost ten years—right around the time I aged out of my parents' insurance. Dr. Pinkerton explained how even minor heart conditions can be exacerbated during pregnancy. So because of the cyst and my heart condition, she "incysted" on seeing me again. HAHAHA! I'm sorry, I couldn't help myself. They scheduled an echocardiogram to check my valve.

Two weeks later, we were back for the echocardiogram and another ultrasound. Great news—the cyst was shrinking! Not so great news—my mild heart condition had turned to moderate, and Dr. Pinkerton strongly urged me to plan to deliver in this larger hospital (one hour from home) where there were more doctors available in case of emergency.

My heart sank as I pictured a sterile hospital room in place of the deluxe birthing suite we had toured. Craig's heart sank when he learned there would be no hot tub for him to unwind in while I was in labor.

Three weeks later, we were back for yet *another* ultrasound. I didn't mind all these extra appointments because it meant more pictures of our baby! I guess I should thank the cyst after all, which, by the way, was now completely gone!

As it turns out, there was a *lot* more to thank the cyst for. Okay—to thank GOD for! It ended up playing a life-saving role for me and the baby. Here's what happened.

At around twenty weeks, while at one of my ultrasound appointments, a specialist from the University of Minnesota (U of MN), two hours from where we lived, happened to be doing her bi-monthly visits. She literally was walking by as Dr. Pinkerton was looking over my chart. She happened to notice something about a "heart condition" and asked to take a peek.

I remember sitting in Dr. Pinkerton's office when she brought in Dr. Yasuko Yamamura. She introduced herself as Dr. Ya-Ya and told me she's a specialist who delivers babies in high-risk situations at the U of MN. *High-risk? But I'm barely moderate,* I thought. Then I realized she probably just heard I was giving away free snacks, so I offered cheese balls. She giggled as she walked out the door. A few minutes later, both doctors came back. They just couldn't get enough cheese balls!

Actually, I'm kidding. They had come back to discuss something that caught Dr. Ya-Ya's eye. While my valve was only moderately affected by the aortic stenosis, there was a possibility that my aortic arch (the candy cane-shaped part of a major artery called the aorta that comes off the top of the heart and carries blood out to the rest of the body) had become enlarged, which is called an aortic aneurysm. *Yikes! That doesn't sound very good!*

The images Dr. Ya-Ya was looking at from my most recent echocardiogram only showed pictures of my valve, not the aorta above it. She compared it to seeing only part of the map, up to the crease where it's folded over. "We need to get a good picture of the whole map to know what we're dealing with," she said. She recommended a trip to the hospital at the U of MN to get *another* echocardiogram and meet with the cardiologist there.

At least the cyst was gone, I told myself. *But this is getting a lot more complicated than the idyllic natural birth plan I had drawn up.*

The first thing Craig and I did was get people praying. Good idea. The second thing I did was Google: "Aortic Aneurysm." That was a very bad idea. In simple terms, the walls of the aorta get thinned out, and if they get too thin or put under too much pressure, the walls can tear or rupture, which most often is fatal since you lose too much blood too fast. Picture a balloon that bursts open when it gets filled with too much water or air. In pregnancy, a woman's volume of blood is doubled, increasing the risk of an aneurysm rupturing due to more stress on the heart and blood vessels. The third thing I did was start planning my funeral. Okay, I hadn't spiraled that far, but remember—I *was* pregnant which also meant double the hormones, double the emotions, and double the tears. Poor Craig.

What a trooper, though. He always listened empathetically but also had a way of bringing peace and perspective. No surprise that his name means "steadfast."

My "steady Eddie" and I made the two-hour trip to the U of MN hospital. After getting the echo, we met my new cardiologist, Dr. Martin. She was so kind and personable and incredibly sensitive as she shared the not-so-good news. She explained to me that my aortic arch should be measuring around 2-2.5 cm in diameter. According to the preliminary reading, mine was 4.3 cm, meaning I did have an aortic aneurysm that would need to be closely monitored to prevent bursting. *Gulp.*

The narrowing of my aortic valve was causing the blood to shoot through at a faster velocity than normal. She compared it to when you put your thumb over the end of a hose. The same amount of water is forced through a smaller opening. Over time, the force of blood shooting through my aorta has stretched out my artery wall to create a balloon or aneurysm.

I've blown up enough balloons in my life to know they can withstand only so much pressure and then...

Pop.

Dr. Martin reassured me by explaining that while mine was definitely larger than usual, she was not overly concerned. "We start to get nervous when it gets to be 4.5 cm, and open-heart surgery is a must if it gets to 5 cm." She told me *for now* I could still plan to deliver at the hospital one hour from our house, but they would continue to monitor my heart. She scheduled me for another echo six weeks out and prescribed some blood pressure medication to help minimize any further stretching of the artery.

I remember the first night I took the pills. I nearly fell asleep while eating dinner. I literally could not hold my head up. I salted my green beans with tears as I complained to Craig about my total exhaustion. You can imagine my dismay when several weeks later Dr. Martin called and said she wanted to increase my sleeping pills—I mean heart medication. The official reading of my echo came back which showed the measurement had increased to 4.6 cm.

Ummm…remember when she said she starts to get nervous at 4.5 cm? If my cardiologist is nervous—how should I be feeling!? Dr. Martin told me I would need an MRI but didn't want to schedule it until I was in the third trimester—making it safer for the development of the baby.

So now I had questions about how "safe" an MRI was for my baby, but this time I *didn't* turn to Google. (Aren't you proud of me?!) I turned to God. He wasn't surprised by any of this, and even though I was still anxious and worried, I figured He'd bring more comfort than the Internet.

I remember waddling into the white room, hospital gown on and cheese balls ready to dispense. "I'm supposed to go in *that*?" I asked, staring at the giant white tube. "And lay on my back for how long without moving? " (Pregnant ladies DON'T lay on their backs—at least not this far into pregnancy!)

"It should only take about ten minutes," the technician assured me. "And you can listen to whatever radio station you want," he said as he handed me a giant pair of headphones. He helped me onto the cold, sterile, conveyor-belt-type thing and asked if I was claustrophobic. "Nope!" I proudly replied with my headphones and a big smile.

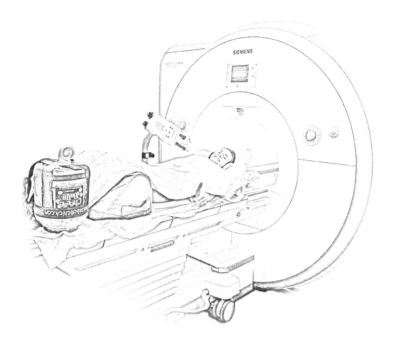

He pushed a button that sent me slowly into the tube. *Can I change my answer?!* I thought as I found myself encased in a tomb that nearly touched my nose and belly. It wasn't long before I learned why they *really* gave me headphones. They were trying to protect my ear drums from bleeding!

Never could I imagine that a high-tech machine in the 21st century would produce sounds so ridiculously loud and obnoxious like an amplified fax machine on steroids. It began its cadence ...Beep! Beep! B-b-b-b-b-beep! Beeeeeeeeeeeep! Grrrr-rrrrrrr!!!!! Honk! Honk! Chitty Chitty Bang! Bang! Rama lama lama ka dinga da dinga dong.

I could hardly hear the music anymore, but I could at least tell when the songs began and ended. So, after four songs, I knew I'd been in there nearly twenty minutes. The anxiety started to creep in, and I found myself cycling through scary scenarios in my mind. *Something must be wrong. I've been in here too long. What if I die? Will my baby survive? I should give Craig my blessing to remarry. Wait. I take that back. No. It's OK. No. It's not. He should be happy. But how could he be happy without ME?!*

And then, a still small voice cut through the chaos.

"Molly, be still."

"Is that You, God?"

"No," the technician answered over the microphone. "We need you to do your best to stay still and not move. There are a couple more pictures we need to get."

"Okay," I whimpered.

"Shouldn't be much longer," he lied. "Are you doing okay?"

"Yes," I lied back.

My poor baby didn't have headphones, and judging by the kicking and punching from within, wasn't a fan of the beeps and bangs either. Since I could barely make out the worship songs on the Christian radio station I requested, I thought I'd try to quote Scripture. But as soon as I got one or two words in, the annoying noises threw me off. I couldn't move. I couldn't concentrate. I couldn't even quote a simple Bible verse. I was nearly crying.

And just as I was ready to give up, I heard another still small voice—aka the Holy Spirit—who happens to have really good ideas. "Quote Scripture to the beat of the MRI machine."

Weird as the idea seemed, at this point, anything to distract me was worth a try. "Trust in the Loooooooooooooorrrrrrrrrrrd with all all all all all your heart-t-t-t-, and leaaaaaaannnnn not on your own under-er-er-er-er-er-er-er-er-standing. In all your ways acknowledge Himmmmmmmmmmm, and He-He-

He-He-He-He (that was me laughing!) will direct your paths. Prov-ov-ov-ov-ov-overbs 3:5-6"

Wow! This is fun! I giggled to myself. And I continued on with quoting all the verses I could remember to the erratic beat of the MRI machine. Thirty minutes later (I'm not kidding!), when they finally took me out, I was tempted to ask to be put back in. I was having the best worship experience of my life, after all!

Truly, that wasn't an exaggeration. I got to experience firsthand how God's Word comforts, guides, and brings peace. All those verses I memorized decades earlier in our church's Awana program and Sunday school came back just when I needed them. I literally went from crazy to calm, from fearful to cheerful, from restless to rejoicing, from worried to worshipping.

I'm so thankful I obeyed the prompting from God to meditate on Scripture. That prepared me for what I was about to hear from Dr. Martin. She broke the news that my aortic aneurysm was now at 4.7 cm, and she no longer felt comfortable with me delivering at the hospital closer to home.

"Your heart just can't take the immense strain of labor," Dr. Martin explained. "So you will need to deliver here at the U of MN, two to five weeks early via scheduled C-Section. That way, surgeons will be standing by in case your aorta tears or ruptures during delivery and they can immediately intervene."

Open heart surgery was imminent, she told me, and might need to happen as soon as I delivered my baby. She also wanted to prepare me that I would likely have to deliver on the East Bank—a part of the hospital where babies could not stay, in order to prioritize my potential emergency situation. I held it together until I heard her say that my newborn and I might be separated by the Mississippi River for the first several days, the days that matter the most for bonding with your baby!

I couldn't imagine being separated from my newborn, not to mention having open heart surgery immediately following a C-Section delivery. I didn't feel cut out for this. (Get it?)

Dr. Martin was so gracious, kind, and empathetic. She waited patiently for me to compose myself enough to ask all the questions swirling in my brain. The silver lining of our conversation was that *if* there was no further enlarging of the aorta, she would give me the green light to deliver on the West Bank where my baby and I could stay together. She scheduled a CAT scan (Great! I love cats!) for three weeks later. Imagine my surprise and disappointment when I entered another white sterile room with another huge tube and worst of all, not a single cat! Fortunately, I was much more mentally, emotionally, and spiritually prepared this time and handled it like a champ.

Great news—it was holding steady at 4.7 cm. One final echo a few weeks later revealed the same good news, and I got the go ahead to deliver on the West Bank. Then came the exciting and totally unexpected part of picking our baby's birthday.

I find it just a bit ironic that *nothing* about my original birth plan panned out, yet we got to *plan* the day and time our child would be born. I guess that's kind of cool! I also think back to the tears I shed and the fret I felt over the cyst. That felt like ages ago! And yet, if it weren't for that cyst, that got me to the next-level

hospital, that led to Dr. Ya-Ya (who
ended up delivering our baby!),
that got me to Dr. Martin,
there is a pretty good chance I
wouldn't be here to write
this book.

Spoiler alert. I
survived! And so
did our baby! There's
actually a whole other
super sweet story all
about this baby, so don't
skip the next chapter!

My aortic aneurysm
held steady through not one
birth but two! Dr. Martin was
quite confident I'd need sur-
gery to repair it before having more kids, but after being followed
closely for ten years, it has not peaked past 4.7 cm. What can I
say? I'm an overachiever. Or in this case, since it hasn't grown—
an underachiever.

The latest guess is that surgery will likely happen in the next
two to five years. If and when it does, I'm quite confident it will
provide ample material for another God story and ample opportunities to trust in the Looooooooooorrrrrrrrrrdddd.

So do you have a heart condition? Maybe not a physical one,
but if you've ever been scared or worried like me, I think that
counts. And while we may be tempted to classify fear and anxiety
as "mild," if we let it go untreated, it can turn to "moderate," and

worse than that, "pretty severe." I discovered the best remedy to a restless heart while in the MRI machine. Simply speak Scripture. Start there. Then be sure to invite others in, giving them the opportunity to empathize and encourage.

> **God's Word says...**"Great peace have those who love Your law, and nothing can make them stumble." (Psalm 119:165)

Let's Talk to God...

God,

Thank You for the promises in Your Word and the peace they bring. When my heart grows fearful, remind me of Your faithfulness. Help me trust in You, Lord, with all my heart-t-t-t-t-. *Amen.*

It's Your Turn!

Below are some of my favorite Scriptures to memorize, and a great place to start if you're new to this. Look up the passages and make a mark by what you want to memorize. I can't wait for God to b-b-b-b-rrrrrrring it to your mind when you need it most. (Sorry, I had to.)

- ❑ Joshua 1:9
- ❑ Psalm 25:4-5
- ❑ Psalm 34:18
- ❑ Psalm 37:4
- ❑ Psalm 139:14
- ❑ Proverbs 3:5-6
- ❑ Isaiah 40:30-31
- ❑ Jeremiah 29:11-13
- ❑ Micah 6:8
- ❑ Matthew 11:28
- ❑ John 14:6
- ❑ Romans 10:9
- ❑ Romans 15:13
- ❑ 2 Corinthians 5:17
- ❑ Ephesians 2:8-9
- ❑ Philippians 4:6-7
- ❑ 1 Thessalonians 5:17
- ❑ 2 Timothy 3:16-17
- ❑ Hebrews 4:14-16
- ❑ 1 Peter 5:7

Chapter 9

Our Little Poppy Seed

ASSUMING YOU READ the last chapter, you know all about my heart condition. Without the divine intervention of a cyst (true story) and Dr. Ya-Ya, it could have become deadly. Now that you're all caught up on the scary part of that pregnancy, I think you'll appreciate this story even more.

When Craig and I found out we were pregnant, we immediately started brainstorming names. We instantly gravitated to boy names, both feeling like we were having a boy. Samuel, Sullivan, Sylvester, Stallone (gotchya!). I liked "S" names to go with our last name, Sanborn. Craig liked...well, he liked names I didn't like.

Realizing we had a lot of time to pick out names for our little man, my focus shifted to my new baby app called Baby Center[1] I found and downloaded. After entering the key information, the app calculated my due date: November 26th, 2012, and sent me a welcome message: "Congratulations! You are four weeks along,

---

1 "BabyCenter." Babycenter.com, app version 4.22.22. https://apps.apple.com/us/app/pregnancy-tracker-babycenter/id386022579 (accessed on July 2, 2022)

and your baby is the size of a poppy seed." *That's unbelievable!*
I thought. My body was already going through changes, and the
baby was no bigger than the period at the end of this sentence.

By week five, the baby was the size of a sesame seed, and just
one week later, our little squirt was the size of a lentil bean…with
a heartbeat! While "Sesame" and "Lentil" or "Little Bean" could
have been cute nicknames, "Poppy" stuck. When we shared the
news of our pregnancy with friends and family, we introduced
the baby as "our little poppy seed." One of my dearest friends,
Roxanne, gave me a sweet congratulatory card with a little
container of—you guessed it—poppy seeds! My mother-in-law
painted a cute stone for our garden with the word "Poppy" on it,
and my mom gave me a beautiful red poppy flower to plant in
my garden. Wait a minute! I never knew poppies were flowers! I
just thought they were seeds on my muffin. It was
adorable to see all the creative ways my friends
and family were showing their excitement for
our baby to be born in November.

Little Poppy was growing fast, and you
better believe I posed each week with
the proper fruit or veggie. From fig, to
lime, to peapod, to lemon, to apple, to
avocado, to turnip, to bell pepper, to
tomato, we were on a roll, and I have the
pictures to prove it! At twenty weeks, our
little guy was as long as a banana and ready
for the big reveal. While neither Craig nor I
are trained ultrasound techs, we had a pretty good idea we were
looking for um, well, a small banana on the bigger banana.

Our eyes were glued to the monitor, and while we were still looking for the little banana, the technician interrupted our quest to announce we were having a girl! After failing to convince her we were having a boy, we began to embrace the evidence and readjust to this new reality. Our little poppy seed was actually a little princess. And we were quite excited. It wasn't that we *wanted* a boy more than a girl, we just thought we were *having* a boy.

After stopping by the mall to pick out our daughter's first official outfits, we headed for home. We threw out one name after another, but nothing sounded right to us. I continued to take pictures with obscure fruits and veggies, as dictated by the updates on my baby app. It was fun to think of our baby being the size of a carrot, a spaghetti squash, a mango, an ear of corn, and a rutabaga.

By the way, what even is a rutabaga?!

When our little Poppy was around the length of a scallion, my app told me she was able to hear my voice and those around me. I guess that means she heard us shouting baby names back and forth as we were riding our bikes through the wooded trails in Lutsen, Minnesota. Someone told us that yelling names could be helpful to determine if it fits or not, so we decided, why let a good bike trip go to waste? "Scarlet!" "Savannah!" "Samantha!" "Summer!" "Sadie!" "Skyler!"

"Psycho!" yelled the biker passing us on the left.

The little human inside me was approaching the size of an eggplant, which did not sound very appetizing. In fact, the other thing that didn't sound good to me was every single baby name. Then, it dawned on me. The reason no name sounded right was because I (and everyone else!) had been calling the baby, Poppy.

The nickname had taken on a life of its own at that point, and it wasn't helping us imagine other names for our little girl.

I soon had to admit that our baby's in-utero nickname had turned into my leading favorite girl name. I liked the name, Poppy. No, actually, I *loved* the name Poppy, but I was pretty sure my hubby did not. So, one night, I mustered up the courage to admit my epiphany to Craig. Embarrassed, I lay in bed next to him with the covers pulled completely over my head and confessed my new favorite name. As expected, he had not been awakened to the wonder of this name. He voiced concern over the possibility of her being teased. He explained, "I don't want people to confuse her with a Hispanic daddy (papi)....and I surely don't want kids to call her "Poopy!"

Craig could tell I was not being persuaded, so he said he *might, possibly, at a later date,* be okay with it as a middle name. "What about Joy as a first name?" he suggested "and Poppy *possibly* as the middle name?" He continued. "Joy Poppy," I said out loud. Something about it felt good, but not completely right. Until ...I reversed it. *Poppy Joy.* Poppy Joy. Poppy Joy! That's it! I felt it. I knew it! Yes. But no ...Craig was not feeling it.

That's when I did something totally out of character, and something that makes me proud to this day. I was quiet. Really. I was. I didn't argue or pester him or whine or lobby or bring it up repeatedly or ask him if he was changing his mind about this name. I zipped my lips, except not with one person. I decided to bug God instead of my husband. The Bible actually says God's okay with that. Isn't that nice? Good to know, right? I prayed that God would work His wonder and woo Craig with the name, Poppy Joy. Praying that God would help us pick out our daughter's name was nothing new. We'd been doing that all along. Now I was just getting really specific with my personal prayers! My specificity took on a new level when I decided to secretly pray that we would not only meet someone named Poppy, but that it would be while on our upcoming trip to Scotland.

Speaking of secrets, Craig was about to turn forty, and for months I had been planning an epic surprise trip to his dream destination. We were able to sneak it in right before I was too close to my due date. After two flights and little sleep, we rented a manual car (oops) which Craig managed to drive on the left side of the road (mostly) as he sat on the right side of the car and navigated what seemed like a thousand roundabouts. Sometimes we circled the same one multiple times until we were dazed and dizzy! It's a miracle we survived!

We arrived at our first lodging late at night. We were greeted the next morning by a field of beautiful red poppy flowers outside our bedroom window! Thank You, God! I bolted out the door, dragging Craig and the camera behind me. While cradling my baby belly, I gracefully squatted next to the flowers for a photo op. Now that I knew poppies were in bloom, I was on a mission to find more red poppy fields in Scotland!

Our next destination was a quaint little cottage called the Carndaisy House in the middle of nowhere, which explains why it took forever to find it. We stayed with a family, but only met the married couple. They must have trained their kids to not disturb the guests because the only peep we ever heard was one of them calling for their puppy. It was strange, though, because we never saw a dog.

On our last full day, we decided to visit DunRobin Castle, an hour's drive away. As we neared the castle, we passed through a tiny town with cute cobblestone roads. Craig slammed on the brakes—which was not abnormal due to wandering sheep—but this time it was because of a sign that read "Poppy's Coffee Shop!" We parked across the street, and I admired each letter of P-O-P-P-Y painted on the white sign that hung above the door. We decided to go to the castle first so as not to miss our tour. We agreed to save what I knew would be the best for last on our way back to the Carndaisy House.

We had a delightful tour of the castle and grounds. Actually, it was not delightful. Craig and I got into a BIG argument because according to him, I was taking too many pictures. I totally disagreed. I had only taken 1,322 pictures since we arrived in Scotland five days earlier. There were many photos I didn't take, I pointed out. The tension between us was building, and Craig's frustration with all my photo requests was growing (Can you blame him?). I was equally frustrated with his lack of enthusiasm for the picture-perfect scrapbook I was planning (Can you blame me? Don't answer.). Things came to a head when I asked him to pose with me for a self-timed picture in front of the castle. He huffed and rolled his eyes as mine filled with tears. I started walking away, but he insisted on the photo op. "We're taking the picture." he said.

"No, we're not." I rebutted.

"I'm standing here until we take the picture." he asserted. So we took the picture. Then it started to rain which matched our moods quite well.

The tension continued as we drove away from the castle. Fortunately, my sweet husband had the wisdom and humility to pull over to the side of the road so we could talk things out. He listened patiently as a I bawled like a baby, talking about how it was the only day in the last six months of pregnancy that I actually felt pretty since I had curled my hair and was wearing a brand-new maternity dress. Then I took my turn and listened to his perspective. He didn't bawl like a baby or talk about being pretty, but he did share that while I was working overtime to capture every moment, he didn't feel capable of just enjoying the moment. We patched up our disagreement with a compromise, a prayer, and a rainbow. Really—after we said "Amen," we opened our eyes to see a vibrant rainbow spread across the sky. What a way to seal the end of our kerfuffle! Isn't God so nice?! Needless to say, this "beautiful" photo of us in front of the castle is not the cover of my scrapbook since our smiles were fake and the struggle was real. But we can laugh about it now—and so can you!

Had we not had to manage a marital conflict, we might have made it to Poppy's Coffee Shop before it closed. (Insert sobbing, deep wailing, partial hyperventilating, and lots of snot.) As I stood under the sign and posed for yet another pregnancy photo (Isn't Craig such a great guy?!), I revealed my secret prayer to my hubby as the tears started flowing again, "I prayed that we would meet someone named Poppy in Scotland,

and this coffee shop was surely going to accomplish that, except now, here we are, and we'll never know who Poppy is!"

After spending our last night at the Carndaisy House, Dougie, the owner, was checking us out in the kitchen. No—not that kind of checking out. We were paying our bill and checking out. As I caressed my big belly, I asked if he knew anywhere along our route to the coast where we might find some more poppy fields. He looked a little puzzled at my question, since most tourists focus on the castles and gorgeous scenery. I told him that Poppy was our baby's nickname, and that I actually liked the name, but Craig didn't. The hugest smile imaginable spread across Dougie's face as he said, "That's interesting you ask, because our daughter's name is Poppy!!"

"WHAT?!?" I accidentally yelled in his face. He didn't have time to respond as I launched into a passionate monologue about our five-month relationship with the name Poppy. Of course, I *had* to tell him about the prayer, which was providential because it opened the door to be able to encourage him in his faith. Turns out he and his family had felt a bit like loners in their commitment to the Lord. How sweet that we got to bring some inspiration and confirmation that God is alive and well.

But back to Poppy! I begged Dougie to let us meet this young, superstar daughter of his. He laughed as he told us that she was fifteen and in school for the day. Then he told us we'd been staying in the room next to hers for the last three nights! Now the puppy-calling all made sense. They were calling for their daughter, Poppy, but their Scottish accent sounded just like "Puppy."

I pelted him with questions. "Does she like her name?" Yes. "Has she ever been called, Poopy?" No. "Is this a common name in Scotland?" No. "Has anyone ever mistaken her for a daddy or grandpa?" No. At this point Dougie interrupted the interrogation and said he would like to tell us the inspiration behind his daughter's name. He told us that he had grown up in a town an hour north, near DunRobin Castle. He lived next door to a sweet woman named Poppy, and she was so kind and loving that he and his wife named their daughter after her. "Now come to think of it," he said, "the town has a coffee shop named after this woman."

No way.

Just when I thought the story couldn't get any better, he nonchalantly reported that their daughter's middle name was...drum roll please...Joy. At this point, I was on the floor about to go into labor. Okay, I might be slightly exaggerating, but I'm pretty sure I was feeling contractions, or perhaps that was just *our* Poppy Joy jumping for joy over hearing confirmation of *her* name.

At this point, Poppy and I were definitely on board with the name, but what about my hubby? His body language had been 100 percent opposite of mine as he sat on a kitchen stool shaking his head and rolling his eyes. But wait, was that a small smirk I noticed?

I showed self-control and waited to attack—gently inquire of his thoughts—until we said our proper goodbye to our host and got into our car. Self-control could only be seen in the rearview mirror as we pulled away from the Carndaisy House. I couldn't hold it in. I slapped Craig's leg until it turned purple. "What do you think? What do you think?" I literally held my breath so he would have a second to respond. He simply, yet so profoundly, said, "It's not like God is saying it's *okay* to name her Poppy Joy. He's saying that her name *is* Poppy Joy." Bring on the goosebumps and celebratory somersaults from Poppy!

Our precious Poppy Joy was born at thirty-eight weeks, measuring as long as a leek—19.5 inches to be exact. Because of my heart condition, I had to deliver two weeks early by C-section. Everything went smoothly, and we got to meet Poppy Joy face-to-face on

November 12, 2012. She also made her debut as the "Cheese Ball Chicklet" matching me with a peanut butter jar full of snacks. P.J., as her dad likes to call her, is as sweet and beautiful as a poppy flower. She loves her name, and besides her little brother, no one else has ever called her "Poopy!"

Each time I reflect on this story, I shake my head in wonderment as I remember that my God is *this* intimately acquainted with each one of us! He knows the number of hairs *on* our heads (Luke 12:7) and all the thoughts *in* our heads (Psalm 139:2). He takes such delight in hearing from us and going above and beyond in answering our prayers (Ephesians 3:20).

Wherever you are in life, wherever you go—God sees you, He calls you, and He knows your name. And make no mistake about it, even though you've grown past the cute and cuddly baby stage, He *still* ooos and awes over you with thoughts more precious than you could imagine.

God's Word says... "Thank You for making me so wonderfully complex! Your workmanship is marvelous—how well I know it. You watched me as I was being formed in utter seclusion, as I was woven together in the dark of the womb. You saw me before I was born. Every day of my life was recorded in Your book. Every moment was laid out before a single day had passed. How precious are Your thoughts about me, O God. They cannot be numbered! I can't even count them; they outnumber the grains of sand! And when I wake up, You are still with me!" (Psalm 139:14-18 NLT)

Let's Talk to God...

God,

Thank You for making me and for knowing my name. Thank You for thinking good thoughts about me and for continuing to love me unconditionally even when I don't feel very lovable. Thank You for having good plans for my life. Help me recognize any lies I've been believing about myself and about You. Please remind me of the truth. *Amen.*

It's Your Turn!

If you are over the age of zero, you've probably believed a lie or two about your worth and value, your purpose, and God's plan for your life. Perhaps you've also believed lies about who God is. Read the following truths (from the Bible) *out loud*. Underline the ones that you need to be reminded of today.

TRUTH

I am loved. (Romans 8:35)

I am forgiven. (1 John 2:12)

I can be strong because of Christ. (2 Corinthians 12:10)

I am a masterpiece. (Ephesians 2:10)

I am created for good works. (Ephesians 2:10)

I have a home in heaven. (Philippians 3:20)

I can be complete in Christ. (Colossians 2:10)

I am chosen. (1 Thessalonians 1:4)

I am a child of God. (1 John 3:1)

I am not condemned. (Romans 8:1)

I do not need to fear. (Isaiah 41:10)

I am wonderfully made. (Psalm 139:14)

God is working in me. (Philippians 2:13)

God is with me. (Psalm 73:23)

God gives me wisdom. (James 1:5-6)

God gives peace. (Philippians 4:7)

God is compassionate. (Psalm 145:8)

God offers an abundant life. (John 10:10)

God goes before His people. (Deuteronomy 31:8)

God is love. (1 John 4:8-10)

God rewards those who seek Him. (Hebrews 11:6)

God fights for His people. (Exodus 14:14)

God hears the prayers of the righteous. (1 Peter 3:12)

God can make me a new creation. (2 Corinthians 5:17)

Chapter 10

S'more on the Door

WE HEARD VOICES as we approached the top of the basement stairs. *That sounds like fighting,* I thought. As my husband and I tentatively descended the steps, we heard what sounded like gun shots coming from below. Just as we were about to duck and cover, Craig recognized the voice of our country's greatest hero—Captain America.

How did the homeowners know Craig's favorite movie was *The Avengers*? Did they suspect it would ultimately seal the deal on us wanting to buy this house? Sneaky ploy, if you ask me!

I already knew this was our future house before even entering. As we turned onto the street, I noticed a playground, volleyball court, basketball court, tennis courts, outdoor theater, baseball fields, a skatepark, and a hockey rink. Though Poppy was barely a year old, and our son was in utero, I had no problem picturing them playing at the park across the street.

"And is that an outdoor pool!?" I blurted out to the realtor. She nodded yes and smiled proudly at her find. "All I need now is a huge tree in the backyard for a treehouse," I said. It was actually written down on my list of hopes and dreams for a house. I had already been praying about that, so as we pulled into the driveway, I felt God smiling as I noticed the towering branches of a massive maple tree spreading out from behind the house.

I didn't even need to see the inside. This was our house. But Craig wasn't convinced yet. That's why I will be forever grateful to Captain America and the rest of earth's mightiest heroes for the clincher. That was just what Craig needed. Now he could envision cuddling on the couch with his incredible, amazing, talented, lovely, beautiful—okay, okay—you get the point—wife, snacking on popcorn, and watching his superhero movies.

We were ready to sign on the dotted line. There was just one problem. Craig needed a job. Well, he had a job, but that was two hours away from this house. That would be a long commute! The reason we were house hunting is because he was nearing the end of the interview process to be the high school youth pastor for a church in the Minneapolis area.

From what we could tell, it seemed they were leaning toward Craig, but we knew there were other highly qualified candidates. We could be days or months away from hearing an answer, and there was no guarantee. So just in case, we decided to casually look at a few houses and start the loan approval process. We definitely did not expect to fall in love so quickly with a house, and we definitely did not plan to try to buy a house before knowing if Craig was hired.

Oops. That's kind of what happened, but not without jumping some major hurdles. I scrambled (not eggs) to get all our documents together for the bank. This would be our first home purchase together, and I was completely clueless as to how loans worked. Can't I just flash a smile, offer them a cheese ball, and tell them we are honest, hardworking, and committed to paying our mortgage bill each month? I quickly discovered that I would rather walk barefoot to Mexico on a path of LEGO bricks than spend time on loan approval paperwork. *By the way, why am I the one doing this?*

I remember sitting in a financial planner's office with Craig when we first got married. I was clueless as to how investing worked and didn't even know what an IRA was or what it stood for. You can imagine my relief as I watched my brand-new husband nod and say "mmm-hhhh" after everything the planner said. *Phew! At least one of us gets it!* I thought, feeling thankful for a financially savvy hubby.

When we got in the car, I asked him to explain all that mumbo jumbo to me. "Oh, I have no idea," Craig nonchalantly shared. "I checked out after about a minute of not understanding."

"Then why did you act like you knew what she was talking about!?" I asked. Craig admitted he was uncomfortable and wanted to get out of there as soon as possible." Needless to say, we had to go back for a second round, so *I* could ask all the questions I thought *he* knew the answers to. Now we know, Craig gets lightheaded anytime he has to deal with the three M's: mathematics, money, or mortgage!

So, to avoid any fainting spells, I was the one who spent hours gathering documents to prove that we could afford the mortgage.

We were told Craig's current income was not enough, so we'd need to rely on our speaking engagement honorariums to supplement. Turns out the bank wasn't confident that was a sustainable income, so they told us to go back to the drawing board. The path to Mexico made of LEGO bricks suddenly sounded very appealing!

Meanwhile, other people had fallen in love with *our* house (I was already a little possessive) and rumor had it their offer was about to be accepted. I wrote a personal and heartfelt letter to the homeowners ~~begging~~ kindly asking them to consider selling the house to us. To paraphrase...We can't buy it quite yet, because, um, yeah, we don't have the money (or job), but we think we will get it, but we're not sure, so yeah, if you could just trust us...Thanks, the Sanborns.

Our realtor hustled to get the letter in the hands of the homeowners, and we prayed and anxiously waited to hear back. It would truly be a miracle if they passed up a solid offer to wait on our ambiguous situation. We knew that if God determined this was the best house and neighborhood for us, that He could make it happen.

In fact, as I'd been praying, God reminded me of the story of how He guided the Israelites from place to place in the wilderness. He led them by a pillar of fire by night (wow—that's so cool to imagine!) and a cloud by day. Where the cloud stopped, they stopped. He knew just the right spot for them, and He knew just the right spot for the Sanborns. He knew just what neighbors we should have for this next phase of our lives.

I couldn't see it with my eyes, but I sensed in my spirit that there was a big fluffy cloud above that house. And if I was right, there was no doubt God would pave a way for us to get there.

I was biting my nails and pacing when my parents called to get an update. They had driven by the house earlier to check out this place we were so excited about. I told them the disappointing news about being denied a loan and how there was a solid offer already on the table.

My dad changed the topic to the business property he and my mom owned that burned down to the ground just a month prior. I was semi-annoyed that he changed the subject and wasn't particularly in the mood for an illustration on perseverance rising from the ashes. "Well," Dad continued, "I just checked the mail before driving here, and the insurance check arrived. Guess what!" He didn't give me time to guess what. He kept talking, "It's almost exactly the amount of the sale price on the house you want to buy."

Dad and Mom went on to say that they felt the timing and amount was a little too coincidental to think that God wasn't involved. They prayed about it and offered to put down a cash offer on our behalf and then sell us the house if and when Craig got the new job.

We were absolutely thrilled! We discussed the "what ifs" and decided that if Craig didn't get the job, we would put the house back on the market. If there was any gain, my parents would keep the money. If there was any loss, we agreed to make up the difference. That could be a lot of lemonade stands, but we were committed!

By the time I called our realtor, my nails were nearly chewed off. I jabbered off something about a fire and my parents, and I think she was about to call 911. I slowed down enough to make better sense and put her in touch with my parents. I'm pretty sure she drafted and delivered the fastest purchase offer in the history of real estate, because within an hour they accepted our offer!

Turns out the cloud *was* there! And while our first attempt at a loan wasn't approved, we felt God's approval as He orchestrated all the necessary details to make this house our home. A month later, Craig was offered the job, and we were able to buy the house from my parents. My dad brought an eighteen-inch, giant pen to closing so we could all sign in style!

Confirmation of God's intervention continued as we met our AWESOME neighbors. Poppy had a built-in best friend next door. Tilly is one month older than Poppy and the two are inseparable. Tilly's two older sisters are just as sweet as Tim and Megan, their parents. Their whole family now attends our church, and Greta, their oldest, has asked me to be her mentor.

Speaking of our church, it was about a year after we moved into our house on Memorial Day weekend when our pastor gave away six firepits at a Sunday service. Yes, our church does creative, cool things like this, but there was only one caveat. The firepits were to be used not only for your family's enjoyment but also to bring your neighbors together. As the youth pastor's wife, I planned to defer to others in our congregation for this cool giveaway. However, I couldn't help but think that not only did we *not* have a firepit, but Craig and I had *just* been talking about wanting to get to know our neighbors more.

All but one firepit had been carried off from the stage, and I felt like it was staring at me. It probably was only a few seconds, but it felt like minutes as Pastor Dan scanned the crowd, waiting for the last recipient. I looked at Craig. Craig looked at me. I looked at Pastor Dan. Pastor Dan looked at me. We shrugged simultaneously, and in that moment, I felt I had Craig and Pastor Dan's blessing to go ahead and be the last recipient.

I lugged the huge box down the steps and partway up the aisle, and Craig lugged it the rest of the way home. A few days later, we hosted our first bonfire. Our invitations were a little unique. We put a graham cracker, a piece of chocolate, and a marshmallow in a bag with an attached note that read:

> Here is your s'more on a door.
> We hope this isn't a bore.
> But in hopes to know you more,
> you are invited to our house at 8:34.

I'll never forget setting up the chairs with Craig and wondering if we had too few or too many. We really didn't know if anyone would come.

Imagine our delight when we had to add more chairs! That night provided an opportunity to get to know our neighbors on a much more personal level. The best story of the night was Nick and Shirley sharing their forty-year love story with us.

We continued to host neighbor nights with more creative invitations left on front doors. This one still makes me giggle:

Here is a hot dog bun.
It is a reminder of the fun
you will have if you come
to National Night Out the day after August one.
(We will provide hot dog buns
so just bring your other ones.)

Eventually we started hosting Christmas parties and Bunco nights. (If you haven't played this addictive, fast-paced dice game, give it a roll!) What a joy to have eighty-five-year-old Al, sitting at a table with our five-year-old son, Tal. Each event and casual curbside conversation has allowed us the privilege of getting to know our neighbors more. Yet, we sensed there was another level of kinship untapped, so we prayed about what else we could do to gain deeper connections with our neighbors.

I wrote a prayer in my journal in March of 2020 asking God to give us His creative ideas to encourage and foster friendship at a deeper level with our neighbors. While we have a mailbox in our front yard that says, "Prayer Drop Box" and a giant pegboard sign with Christmas lights that spells, "Shine Jesus Shine," there hadn't been many personal conversations surrounding our personal faith.

Well wouldn't you know—just days after I wrote that in my journal, COVID-19 happened. I suppose it had *been* happening, but no one knew how impactful it was until shutdowns began—including churches! For the first time in our lifetime, there was no church to go to on Sunday. Craig and I decided we should have church at our house for our neighbors.

Remember the toilet paper shortage? I know—you are wondering what this has to do with church—wait for it! Before bathroom tissue became a coveted commodity, I had taken a trip to Costco and secured a giant pack of thirty. While lying in bed one night, Craig and I prayed that God would give us His creative ideas for the invitations and planning of our neighborhood church gatherings. As usual, God delivered. He reminded us of our stockpile of TP, and that played a significant ~~roll~~ role (Get it?!) in inviting our neighbors to church.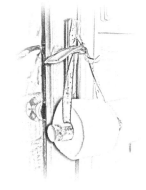

Craig and I stayed up late composing the poem and put it to print the next day. The kids helped us stuff each toilet paper roll with the paper and ribbon so it could be hung on doorknobs.

The message inside read:

Roll on Over!
Our church has been cancelled from COVID-19!
Whether you're religious or not or somewhere between,
We'll open our home to have neighborhood church.
If you're seeking encouragement discontinue your search;
Come as you are for donuts, coffee, and fun!
Sweatpants are welcome at 8601.
We will meet Sunday morning at 10:30.
Soap will be provided if your hands are dirty.
We will scrunch in our living room to laugh, share, & pray.
But no pressure at all to perform in any way.
Fellowship and friends aren't found on Amazon.
So come together as we read from the book of John.
Our goals are two-fold as we combat this virus:
Number one is to wipe away fear through Jesus.
Number two is to come together as a community.
So please don't flush this opportunity!
Whether you come or not, consider this roll a gift.
We trust God can multiply what we have left!
We hope our toilet paper innuendos made you grin—
Now circle all you see, for a prize you may win!

If there is ever another toilet paper shortage that coincides with another shut down (please no!), feel free to use the poem. We are only stewards of God's creativity. He's the author of laughter and fun, and He gets all the credit!

Similar to setting up for that first firepit night, we were unsure what to expect. It's one thing to ask people over for games and food, but for "church" and during a pandemic? Again, we were absolutely thrilled with the turnout, but even more so with the depth of discussion. We kept our word and Craig read from the book of John, did a simple teaching, took prayer requests, and prayed. After our informal yet personable service, our neighbor, Phil, shared that was the best church service he'd ever been to in his eighty years.

As restrictions tightened, we transitioned to church outside—in the tennis courts, actually! I couldn't help but think back almost ten years prior when we drove down our street for the first time. I had no problem picturing us playing tennis across the street, but hosting neighborhood church was not in my dreams. I could never have imagined, but God knew—and I'm pretty sure that's one of the reasons that cloud has stayed steady above our house all these years.

On Easter, we held church in our front yard. Craig explained the significance of Jesus's life, death, and resurrection by using special Bibles with colored tabs. Each person held a Bible, and we took turns reading the verses.

Nick volunteered to read the verse highlighted after the yellow tab, which was Romans 3:23—"All have sinned and fall short of the glory of God."

Shirley thumbed to the black tab, found Romans 6:23, and read, "For the wages of sin is death, but the free gift of God is eternal life in Christ Jesus our Lord."

Arne found the red tab and read to us about God's love from Romans 5:8. "But God demonstrates His own love toward us in that while we were yet sinners, Christ died for us."

We listened to Tim read Ephesians 2:8-9 after he flipped to the blue tab. "For it is by grace you have been saved, through faith—and this is not from yourselves, it is the gift of God—not by works, so that no one can boast."

Vikki found the green tab which led her to Romans 10:9-10. "If you declare with your mouth, 'Jesus is Lord,' and believe in your heart that God raised Him from the dead, you will be saved. For it is with your heart that you believe and are justified, and it is with your mouth that you profess your faith and are saved."

S'mores and hot dogs are great, but God's Word brings encouragement and nourishment for a lifetime. What an honor to partner with God by bringing love and light to our precious neighbors.

And the blessing goes both ways! Nick and Shirley are always willing to share their tools and assist with advice and even manual labor! Adam knows everything automotive and is always willing to help troubleshoot. Sarah gives the best birthday gifts. Clara has a bubbly personality and brings joy to our block. Arne and Carol couldn't be more gracious and tolerant living next to the noise my son produces, not to mention all the Nerf bullets and balls that end up in their yard. Tim has probably cooked my family more dinners than I have myself! Megan holds a warm and good conversation, whether it is in the driveway, yard, or park as we holler at our kids to not get hit by a car. Tilly, Lydia, and Greta are great cat companions and garden tenders when we are away. Nina gives the best Halloween candy. Vikki has a knack for making things look beautiful and making people feel special. Andrea is a great companion and encourager when laying sod or going on walks. Autumn is a super fun and responsible babysitter. Phil and Jeri bought the neighborhood kids a basketball hoop and tag team with Vikki to host "Happy Hour" on Thursdays. For years, Al has been corresponding with neighborhood kids through a special mini mailbox in his yard. He signs his cards from "the little people" so kids believe they are pen pals with the garden gnomes throughout Al's yard. Luana taught Poppy "Jingle Bells" on the piano and gifted me with beautiful yellow primrose to grow in my garden.

Speaking of gifts, Craig outdid himself and planned not one, not two, but *three* surprise parties for my fortieth birthday. The final one was my favorite. Craig gathered all the neighbors and we met at the picnic shelter across the street. The cake was good, but the sweetest treat was when Craig asked everyone to pick one word to describe me. My hubby knows how much words of affirmation mean to me! Sweet and organized Vikki offered to record the list which became my favorite gift of all. One by one, they filled my love tank with heartwarming and humbling words. But I soon noticed a theme develop. Whether it was the word sparkle, shine, bright, or light, the pattern was obvious.

What was perhaps less obvious was that light they spoke of is not me at all. I couldn't be more confident that it is Christ *in* me. I am like a clay pot with cracks and imperfections, and Christ is the light shining beautifully through my brokenness. It is Jesus *in* me they are drawn to!

So how about you? Do you have that light? You don't have to work for it or get all polished up to shine. The verses Craig shared on Easter sum it up. Jesus, the light of the world, is a *free* gift to anyone who receives Him.

God's Word says... "Whoever follows Me will never walk in darkness, but will have the light of life." (John 8:12b)

Let's Talk to God...

Jesus,

Thank you for dying on the cross to pay the penalty for my sin. You defeated sin and darkness when You rose from the dead. Thank You for offering me Your love and Your light. Shine in me and through me and to all those around me. *Amen.*

It's Your Turn!

How shiny are you? (I don't mean oily skin!) Do you have the light of Christ in you, and if so, how brightly is He shining? Ask God to show you how you can shine brighter to those around you and write down what He brings to mind.

If you're feeling a bit in the dark, and you're not sure if this "light" is in you, would you take some time to write down your questions below? Ask God to give you understanding for what it means to accept the free gift of His Son, Jesus, the light of the world. You may want to go back to page 133 and re-read the verses that sum this up.

If those Scriptures just "clicked" for the first time, and you have decided to "declare with your mouth that 'Jesus is Lord' and believe in your heart that God raised Him from the dead" (Romans 10:9), may I be the first to welcome you to the family?! This family of believers includes old and young from the beginning of time, encompasses every culture, and will share a future forever home in heaven! Maybe after we arrive, we can share some s'mores and I can hear *your* story!

But before we get there, here are some quick pointers to help you start your journey with Jesus. These are not things you *have* to do to be a Christian, but things you *get* to do. It's about a relationship, not a religion.

- Tell someone about your decision to follow Christ (pick me! pick me!).

- Find a Bible. I recommend the New International Version (NIV) or the New Living Translation (NLT).

- READ the Bible! I recommend starting in John.

- Start talking to God like you'd talk with a friend.

- Ask God to help you find a good church and get involved.

- Ask God to help you find an older, mature Christian who can encourage you.

Chapter 11

Confessions of Jealousy

I don't want to tell this story. It makes me look bad. Do I have to?

Oh, I'm sorry. You caught me in the middle of a conversation with God. He's not letting me off the hook on this one, so here goes nothing.

I was jealous of someone.

God intervened.

Now I'm not jealous.

The end.

You want more details? Argh. Okay. It makes me look bad, but I'll try again. My kids were stowed securely in back of the minivan. (Not in the trunk! Don't worry, I took the thirty minutes it takes to securely strap them into their car seats.) I was about to pull out of the driveway—running late—of course. But I saw a text come in from my hubby, so I quickly skimmed it.

He said he just stumbled upon an abstinence speaker (that sentence doesn't sound good), and he thought she was awesome.

I thought, *How about me? **I** am an abstinence speaker! Am I awesome?* He said he was very impressed with her content and website. I found myself instantly hot all over. Was this a hot flash? I've heard about those, but I'm pretty sure I was much too young for menopause. He went on and on about all the great resources she had and said he was going to try to book her to speak for his youth group.

He sent me the link to her website, which happened to be her name. I immediately recognized it as someone I had mentored in speaking years ago. Well, I guess if you count meeting at a picnic table for forty-five minutes as mentoring–well, yeah, I did that. This woman had reached out to me to seek advice about speaking. I hadn't heard from her in years, but now here she was coming up in Google searches.

Sitting in my driveway when I should have been heading to church, I started venting to myself. I had been bugging my husband for months to agree to put some money into revamping our website and making it mobile friendly. I wanted to add resources too. Plus, we were guilty of false advertising since our photos were ten years old when my husband's hair was not yet gray, and I had fewer wrinkles. But now, here he was wanting to bring in my understudy to speak. *Ooo. There was that hot flash again.*

And just when I should have been pulling out of the driveway (like ten minutes ago!), I instead pulled up her website. As I scrolled and scrolled and scrolled, I got hotter and hotter and hotter. My kids were in the backseat throwing stale goldfish at my head, telling me to start driving. But I was in a zone, and I was feeling all the feelings. I was in no shape to drive a car.

In hindsight, I can identify my feelings as a shade of envy, but I couldn't admit it then. I pulled out of the driveway and stuffed that little ordeal down deep where it wouldn't bother me anymore...or so I thought!

Several months later, while juggling two young kids (not literally—that'd be funny though!), grad school, and speaking, somehow, I managed to squeeze in a conference in North Carolina. The Set Free Summit was put on by Josh McDowell, an avid advocate for sexual integrity, and one of my heroes.

The goal of the conference was to teach and equip the attendees with tools to help those struggling in addiction and destructive behaviors. Hundreds of passionate, like-minded people with a heart for ministry were congregating in one place. What a privilege to be a part of that!

I went knowing *no one*, but I wasn't too worried, because I had my cheese balls, and they always help break the ice. With snacks strapped to my back and a smile on my face, I joined the hustle and bustle of the exhibit hall. I bounced from booth to booth, making friends as I went.

I kept my eye out for Josh McDowell, because I had this secret desire to meet him. Maybe I would give him a cheese ball and strike up a conversation. Perhaps he would notice something special in me, take me under his wing, and mentor me in speaking. At the very least, I wanted to get a picture with him. Okay, whoa. I definitely didn't admit that to anyone then, but now here I am telling you. I'm a little embarrassed.

After meeting with vendors and picking up some resources, I headed to the cafeteria for our first meal. I scanned the tables for an open seat, and for a few seconds felt like an insecure middle school student looking for a friend. But then I spotted an opening at a table and headed that direction.

And then...I saw her...abbyludvigson.com in the living flesh. *Are you kidding me! Why is she here?* The Holy Spirit answered me and said, "Um, Molly, she's coming to get equipped to help people." I told the Holy Spirit that I could cover the region of Minnesota all by myself.

But at this point, Abby had noticed me too, so I had to continue the course. With an upside-down frown on my face, I greeted her, and we small talked for a minute. I think I may have said something like how nice it was to see her. I added that lie to the list of things I'd need to confess to the Lord later.

When I asked Abby how she ended up hearing about the conference, I figured she'd mention the same email blast I got. "Oh," she said, "Josh invited me." *Josh?...Oh, Josh!...You're on a first name basis with him? I feel Mr. McDowell would have been more appropriate.* And there was that hot flash again. I'm pretty sure steam was coming out of my ears. I glanced at my skin to make sure it wasn't turning green from envy.

I still was holding out hope that she meant he informally and impersonally invited her through an online ad or something. Nope. She went on to tell me she had attended a speaker training he hosted, and he ended up mentoring her and was now helping her get a curriculum and video series launched. *I've always wanted to do a video series*, I thought.

Then I had a really bad thought. I don't want to tell you. I don't want to write it down. Argh. Fine. I will. I thought, *Well, hopefully her curriculum and video series isn't very good.*

At this point, my jealousy turned to disgust. I was disgusted with myself. *Oh, my goodness. How could I, a mature (at least I used to be) follower of Jesus in her thirties, one who claims to care about people, have these terrible feelings? I should be so excited for Abby and the message of sexual integrity and truth that she is spreading to our youth.*

I wanted to curl up in a ball and ask Abby to kick me all the way back to Minnesota. *I deserve to be kicked,* I thought. From jealousy to disgust, I now was experiencing intense shame. I ate as fast as I could and headed straight for my room. As soon as the door closed, I cried. It was a pretty ugly cry. It was a good representation of my heart right about then.

I may have closed the hotel door, but another door flung wide open. My negative thoughts had created an entry for Satan to assault me with lies and condemnation. *And you call yourself a Christian?* he said. *You don't deserve to be here,* he whispered. *You don't deserve to be a speaker. You should just quit doing ministry because your heart is gross. God knows everything you've been thinking, and He will never use you.*

I found myself on my knees, begging God to forgive me. I really didn't need to beg. His Word promises that He already has. I still felt it was important to speak out the hidden sins. I didn't want envy, jealousy, or comparison, to lurk beneath the surface of my heart any longer. I confessed those things, I thanked the Lord for His mercy and grace, and I asked Him to bless Abby and her ministry.

Feeling like it might bring even more freedom, I decided to call my mentor. I knew she'd have some wise words for me. It was no small miracle that she was free right then to take my call and

spend over thirty minutes on the phone with me. I could sense
the heaviness lifting even more as I confessed out loud to her.
I experienced what James 5:16 promises: "Confess your sins to
each other and pray for each other so that you may be healed."
After listening, she led me through a powerful time of prayer. At
the end, she asked me to ask God if there was anything He wanted me to know about or learn from this experience.

I asked the Lord. Then I listened. It's not that I heard it
audibly, but it came through crystal clear in my spirit. "You are
a living fragrance." Whoa. I
thought. Nope, that couldn't
be. Maybe what He meant
to say is "You stink." That's a
statement I could get behind.
But a living fragrance? Truth
be told, that's not the first
time I've heard that phrase.
It's what my name means.
I know this because it was
written on a plaque right under "Molly" and still hangs in
my parent's upstairs hallway.

My siblings teased me when we were kids that the sign meant
that I smell. I never liked the meaning of my name because of it.

Now that you know my history with that phrase, perhaps you
are thinking I just thought it up, and it really wasn't God talking
to me. Believe me, I wrestled with that possibility too. But since
I was not in a place to think anything positive about myself, let
alone a memory from my childhood, I knew it was the Lord.

I still had a hard time accepting it until something quite undeniable happened. On the last day of the conference, I sat down at my seat to find a small gift bag. Everyone had one at their seat as a gift from Josh and Dottie McDowell. I opened it up and found a small perfume bottle. There was a note attached to it that said, "May you become a sweet aroma to all who encounter you." It referenced the same verse my name plaque quotes.

Happy and humble tears filled my eyes as I recognized this as a gift from God. He blessed me when he could have blasted me. He accepted me instead of rejecting me. He spoke life and purpose over me when I had done the opposite. He replaced my envy and gave me excitement for Abby and the work He was doing through her.

In fact, when God led me to write a talk called "Obsessive Comparison Disorder" and share the story at a women's event, I felt I should contact Abby to get permission to share her website as a way to celebrate her work. God nudged me to share the whole story with her. *Seriously, God?!* I protested. *It's one thing to tell You, my mentor, and a group of women, but I should tell HER? That's a whole new level! Haven't I done enough?*

God persisted, and I submitted. My heart was racing as I called Abby—my husband had her number because he had recently booked her to speak. *Hey, God, no hot flashes! Thank you for changing my heart!*

Abby could not have been more kind, gracious, and understanding. She thanked me for my courage to tell her the whole story. I thanked her for her compassion and grace. I'll never forget what she said at the end of our forty-five-minute conversation. "I feel like my heart is knitted to yours." There was no denying it. I felt the same way.

Isn't God funny? Here I am writing a book, promoting the ministry of the very person I was competing against. But I can honestly tell you I am doing this with great joy. There is not a pang of jealousy nor any feelings of competition, and I owe it all to the Lord! In fact, we've become good friends and have so much fun together!

May we daily ask God to search our hearts and redirect our thoughts to reflect Him. I wonder how different this story would be if I had recognized my sin and repented in the minivan that day. If you have neglected it like I did and find a massive mess inside yourself, know that there is a gracious and forgiving God that does a good job cleaning up gross things. I should know!

Oh, and by the way—I did get my picture with Mr. McDowell.

I mean, Josh.

God's Word says... "The Lord is compassionate and merciful, slow to get angry and filled with unfailing love. He will not constantly accuse us, nor remain angry forever. He does not punish us for all our sins; He does not deal harshly with us, as we deserve. For His unfailing love toward those who fear Him is as great as the height of the heavens above the earth. He has removed our sins as far from us as the east is from the west. The Lord is like a father to His children, tender and compassionate to those who fear Him." (Psalm 103:8-13 NLT)

Let's Talk to God...

Dear Lord,

Thank you for Your compassion, kindness, mercy, grace, and forgiveness. Please search my heart and show me if there is anything I need to make right with You or others. Please reveal any hidden sins to me and empower and equip me to turn from them and turn to You for help to overcome. *Amen.*

It's Your Turn!

Since I wrote about my icky sin of jealousy for the world to read, would you be willing to write down whatever God may show you in your life that needs a bit of an adjustment? Take a minute to ask God to bring to your mind any attitudes or behaviors that need some redirection.

Then write out a prayer of confession below and be sure to add a prayer of thanksgiving to God for His forgiveness and unconditional love. If you need some guidance on these kinds of prayers, David does this all throughout the Psalms. (Check out Psalm 51.)

One more thing—can I challenge you to share with a trusted friend or family member? I know from experience that there is a lot of freedom and healing when you "confess your sins to each other." (James 5:16)

Chapter 12

From Peas to Peace

I WAS AWAKENED AT 2 A.M. by the sound of crying. My husband heard it too. Upon recognizing it as our two-year-old son, Tal, we very groggily played "rock, paper, scissors" in bed to see who would go. I should have picked paper to beat his rock, but his rock crushed my scissors. Anyway, as I stumbled down the hallway, I noticed Tal's crying was different than normal. It wasn't a hungry cry. *That's good.* It wasn't a poopy-diaper cry. *Thank you, Jesus!* It wasn't a thigh stuck in the crib cry. *Phew, because we were fresh out of the cooking spray I would need to free his leg!*

It sounded like he was scared. As I approached his crib, I said, in the most quiet, sympathetic voice I could muster, "Buddy, what's wrong?"

He looked up at me with tear-filled eyes and said, "Black lion. Black lion get me."

We hadn't been to a zoo lately, and he hadn't seen *The Lion King.* While it's possible my son was having a random dream about a lion, I decided to treat it like an attack from the prowling lion himself—Satan. (1 Peter 5:8) And that called for some spiritual warfare.

I scooped up my sweet son, and we snuggled in the rocking chair. As he rested, I went to battle. The only weapon I needed was the name of Jesus. So with conviction and confidence, I prayed out loud, "I come against Satan's schemes to frighten Tal and steal his sleep, in the powerful name of Jesus. I pray for peace. Jesus, bring peace. Jesus, please bring peace to Tal."

Tal looked up at me and said, "and apples." I looked at my son, completely confused. *Was he hungry after all?* "And peppers," he added. *What?*

"Tally, we're not going to have a snack right now," I said.

But he continued, "Jesus bring peas, and apples, and peppers." Just as I was about to ask him for clarification, it dawned on me. Tal thought I was asking Jesus to bring peas—not peace. So, it just made sense to him to add a few more items to the shopping order!

I immediately started laughing, which I guess was contagious, because Tal followed suit. The more I laughed, the more he laughed. I don't even think he knew why we were laughing, which made it all the funnier. Tal's tears were gone, but now I had them streaming down my face and was afraid I might pee in my pants!

It took a while for us both to calm down, but when we did, I thanked Jesus for not only bringing peace, but also for bringing joy—and lots of it. As I rocked my sweet Tally-man, I pictured Jesus looking down at me, much like I was looking at my son, with a soft smile and kind eyes.

He looks at you that way, too, you know. And He wants to bring you calm and comfort. That will come when you call on the name of Jesus—and I recommend doing so out loud! There is no other name more powerful than His. Philippians 2:10-11 tells us that "at the name of Jesus every knee should bow, in heaven and on earth and under the earth, and every tongue acknowledge that Jesus Christ is Lord."

I've put this into practice with my daughter, Poppy, as well. I remember the night she woke me up with tears in her eyes and fear in her heart. She had a dream that a skunk was eating her door. I knelt down and empathetically said, "Honey, that really stinks." After we giggled about my cheesy joke, I tapped into the power that comes through calling on the name of Jesus, asking Him to give her good dreams and to help her have a good night's sleep.

Chances are you are dealing with a lot more than a scary dream about a lion or a skunk. Maybe you're living what feels like a nightmare, and perhaps you are loaded down with fear, anxiety, and worry. God's platter of peas—errr—I mean peace, is within arm's reach. To accept it is to simply acknowledge His presence and His power and exchange your fear for His gift of faith, which He gives generously, by the way! (James 1:5)

God's Word says... "Don't worry about anything; instead, pray about everything. Tell God what you need and thank Him for all He has done. Then you will experience God's peace, which exceeds anything we can understand. His peace will guard your hearts and minds as you live in Christ Jesus." (Philippians 4:6-7 NLT)

Let's Talk to God...

Jesus,

Your name is so powerful. Please help me remember to use it in times of trouble and give me confidence to declare it out loud. I give You my fears and ask for more faith. I give You my worries and ask for reminders from Your Word. In Your mighty name, Jesus, *Amen.*

It's Your Turn!

Is there something in your life right now that is causing you to worry or to be afraid?

_____

_____

_____

_____

Would you be willing to give it to God? Sometimes I need a tangible act to help solidify an internal decision. So feel free to drop it in the box next to Tal's lion and Poppy's skunk.

Chapter 13

Broken Hip. Happy Heart.

THERE ARE A PLETHORA of parenting decisions I am *not* proud of, but I must admit there is one that is working beautifully. While spending a weekend away prepping for the upcoming homeschool year with our children, Poppy and Tal, I felt prompted by God to institute a regular time of worship and prayer for our family.

One of my motivations was to curb the chaos and start our day on the right path. Breakfast can be a battle as we must remind our son about twenty-five times to come back to the table. Chores tend to take ten times as long as they should, leaving me feeling frazzled before we've even started our school day.

A routine of worship and prayer gets us grounded. I wish I could tell you that I play the piano or strum the guitar as my kids sing like the von Trapp family in *The Sound of Music*. Unfortunately, the only instrument I dedicated time to learning was the recorder. I know. What was I thinking? Actually, what were my parents thinking to pay for six years of private lessons on a plastic instrument? I joke a lot, but sadly, this is no joke. Ha!

Since all I can remember is "Hot Cross Buns" and the "Irish Washerwoman," we have turned to YouTube for our music. We each pick a song and worship along. Sometimes my son chooses to worship through somersaults and ninja kicks off the couch. When he starts swinging the cat by the tail 'round and 'round, we intervene.

After worship, we go through the P.R.A.Y. acronym. We don't follow the "rules" of having our eyes closed and hands folded. Instead, we take a casual and conversational approach—at least for the first letter.

"P" stands for Praise.

We tell God what we are grateful for.

"God, thank You for our cat. Our neighbors. Our house. Plenty of food in our cupboard." *And right now, I thank God for YOU and that you are reading this book!*

"R" stands for Repent.

Here we *do* ask our kids to find some focus and close their eyes if needed.

We ask God if there is anything we need to make right with Him, with each other, or with others. Then we pause and listen for not more than ten seconds or so. It's been amazing to see what happens during this time. Craig and I have utilized it to seek forgiveness from one another—something that's pretty valuable to do in front of our kids. The sweetest is when Poppy or Tal apologizes to the other. Seeing their tenderness toward one another is a refreshing reminder that they are learning and growing.

Yes, quarreling absolutely occurs at our house, but this routine provides a time to let God search our hearts, evaluate our actions, and make things right.

"A" stands for Ask.

Similar to praise, we call out requests, taking turns talking to God about our desires, needs, and the needs of others.

"God, please help Grandma feel better. Please help us do well in our ninja competition. Please make it snow." (That's a hard ask in June!)

"Y" stands for Yield.

This is the most important part! We say, "God, is there anything You want to say to us or remind us of?" Then we listen.

More often than not, we don't sense the Lord saying anything specific, but sometimes He reminds us of something we've been putting off, brings a Scripture or song to mind, or puts a person on our heart.

One September morning, Poppy reported that she felt God told her we should bring flowers to Al. This was a very specific word from the Lord! Al is an elderly neighbor of ours who had recently lost his wife. He loves gardening and flowers, so this assignment from God sounded right on. I fully intended to dig out a vase and snip some flowers later that day with Poppy, but we put it off.

The next morning during our P.R.A.Y. time, Poppy reported again that God was telling her to bring flowers to Al. "Oh, honey, yes, yes. We need to do that. We will do that," I said.

We didn't do it.

On the third day, Poppy had not forgotten and was growing impatient. "MOM, we NEED to bring flowers to Al!"

"Yes, yes, honey! We will do it," I said with all good intentions. I really thought it would happen. It didn't. And by the way, why am I writing about this? It makes me look SO bad!

On the fourth day, God stayed *consistent* with what He was telling Poppy, and Poppy stayed *persistent* with what she was telling me. After our P.R.A.Y. time, my phone rang. I answered to hear Al's voice on the other end. "Well, hello, Molly. I know your family cares about me, so I thought you may want to know that I fell on Monday and broke my hip. I'm calling from the hospital."

Let me tell you, if I was a turtle, my head would have been inside my shell. If I was a dog, my tail would be between my legs. If I was an ostrich, my head would be in the sand. Get the point? I felt *terrible*. Monday just happened to be four days earlier, the same day Poppy first felt prompted to bring Al flowers. I can't help but wonder if I had listened right away, if there was a chance we could have intercepted Al *before* he fell and broke his hip? Or would we have arrived just after he fell and could have given timely help to our sweet neighbor?

The day Al got home from the hospital, you better believe we snatched the scissors, snipped the flowers, and high-tailed it over to his house. Poppy and I told him the whole story. He was extremely encouraged to know that God spoke to Poppy on his behalf. And then we took time to speak to God right then and there as we prayed for Al and the healing of his hip. His hip may have been broken, but his heart was happy knowing God noticed him. Poppy's friendship with Al and her relationship with God were strengthened on this day.

As for me, I was reminded how important it is to take time to listen to the Lord, because He does indeed speak, even through children, and I need to listen and obey (right away!).

Does this story, by chance, bring to memory any times you were delinquent in responding to God? I hope it's not just me! If something comes to mind, I encourage you to respond to God. And maybe it's not too late. Give them a call. Shoot them a text. Stop by their house. Ask for forgiveness.

I don't know what God's been nudging you to do, but who knows, maybe there's an Al in your life who will be blessed because of your obedience and care.

> **God's Word says...** "Call to Me and I will answer you and tell you great and unsearchable things you do not know." (Jeremiah 33:3)

Let's Talk to God...

Lord,

Thank You for not only listening to me but for also speaking to me. Help me to learn to recognize Your voice and respond right away. Please nudge me to check in with You often. Is there anything You want to tell me now, Lord? *Amen.*

It's Your Turn!

Did you hear anything? If you prayed that prayer, you just asked God if there was anything He wanted to tell you. If He did—write it down!

_____

_____

_____

Also, take a minute to list any outstanding assignments from God you've been neglecting. Then jot a quick note on when and how you will follow through.

Assignment	Follow-Through Plan	Done?
		☐
		☐
		☐
		☐
		☐
		☐
		☐
		☐

Chapter 14

Lost and Found

I STARTED SPEAKING when I was twenty-two years old. I was a late bloomer. Just kidding—not *that* kind of speaking! Public speaking! As God grew this gift in me, it became clear that this was what He called me to do. Finding my life partner, Craig, who also had a passion for speaking and ministry, was just one of many affirmations I've received from God.

By the time we got married, we had been speaking on our own for a combined fifteen years, so learning to share the stage (and microphone) took a little getting used to. Our first speaking engagement together was a month after our wedding when we spoke to middle schoolers for a week at Camp Lebanon in Minnesota. We basically took our own talks and material and told each other what to say when. It was a little wonky, but we quickly discovered that wonky as it was, our audience really liked the husband-wife, tag-team approach.

We continued to have many opportunities to speak which forced us to start writing new material together. This provided us plenty of chances to work on communication and compromising in our marriage. I am proud to say I am really good at communicating my opinions! And Craig is super skilled at rolling his eyes! Jokes aside, we have had to learn to communicate incognito while on stage. We use inconspicuous grimaces, barely audible grunts, and facial expressions to *try* to clue one another in on what we're thinking.

I remember one speaking engagement when I straight-up glared at Craig, only to receive a glare straight back. *How dare he!* I thought. *How dare she!* He thought. I gave him "the look" because he was talking a mile a minute and skipping all the good stuff—including some of *my* parts. He was glaring at me because he thought we were over time as I just kept blabbing on. It turns out he thought we were done at noon, but we actually had another thirty minutes! I can't blame him for scowling at me, though. I have a reputation of trying to fit in more than we have time for, and he is always cognizant of the clock and ending on time. That's one of the many reasons I need Craig in my life!

We've had our ups and downs, but after speaking together for nearly fifteen years, we've found a rhythm. Preparation is not *as* hard as it used to be—still a lot of work, but not as much as before. However, there was a time recently when we really struggled in preparing four messages for a weekend youth retreat at SpringHill in Michigan.

We also were in the middle of preparing and practicing new messages for FamilyLife Weekend to Remember marriage conferences. We had just been invited to join their speaker team and were thrilled for our first event with them.

With our prep time split between two very different events, we hoped and prayed things would come together quickly. They definitely did not. We put more hours into preparing for the SpringHill retreat than normal, which was odd since it was our third time back at this camp, and the first two times were much smoother.

We spent all day Thursday finalizing our messages while our children were at their homeschool co-op. Craig went to his office and put another three hours into his parts of the messages. His eyes were so glazed over and his head so foggy, I can understand why he accidentally selected "Don't Save" when his computer asked him if he wanted to save his document. Fortunately, he had printed a hard copy, so he was able to work from that, though it wasn't ideal since he still wanted to make some changes!

By the time we got on the plane the next morning, we were already exhausted from all the time and effort it took to prepare. We both felt we needed those two hours on the plane to highlight, cross out, add arrows, and make final tweaks to our messages. I literally breathed a sigh of relief as we deplaned. We were *finally* ready!

When we got to baggage, I noticed Craig frantically looking through his backpack. If you know Craig, he's not usually frantic about anything. I hesitantly approached and held my breath. I didn't want to ask if he was looking for the messages because I didn't want my worst fear to be confirmed. I also didn't feel I had the emotional capacity to be a nice wife at that moment, so I tried to live in denial as long as possible.

Craig very sheepishly looked up at me. All four hard copies of his talks had been left in the plane seat pocket. He was sure of it. I clenched my teeth and converted the words I wanted to say into hot air that began to release out of my ears. My cortisol levels shot through the roof from the instant anxiety I felt.

I began to imagine our weekend if we *didn't* get those notes back. We would have to try to remember and re-write *all* of Craig's parts. There went our two-hour leisurely drive in the rental car to camp. Instead of hanging out with teens and handing out cheese balls throughout the weekend, we'd be stuck in our room trying not to get frustrated at each other as we prepared all the messages for a third time.

Honestly, it felt easier to leave Craig at the airport and go do the weekend myself. Maybe he wouldn't notice if I just snuck over to the rental counter. There would be less stress trying to re-do everything, and I wouldn't have to try to be a kind, loving, supportive wife in the midst of being super-duper mad.

Fortunately, God knows my weaknesses and promises to give us what we need when we ask. So, as Craig headed to the information booth to beg for help in getting those precious papers back, I took a deep breath and asked God to give me an attitude adjustment. It could have easily been me that left the notes on the plane, and the best thing I could do would be to show love and grace—like Craig has shown me a million times before. (Like the time I ran over a curb at the airport and blew a tire, or the time Craig had to leave work to help me get my hair out of the power drill, or the time I put his favorite baseball hat in the dryer and shrunk it.) The only silver lining to getting into a big argument in the airport would be that we *could* use that for an illustration for our upcoming marriage conference. There's a window into the mind of a speaker for you!

I texted some close friends and family members and asked them to pray we would find the notes (and that I would be a nice wife). Craig talked to Tammy at information and explained our situation. She was sympathetic and immediately contacted someone to check the plane. They came back empty handed and said the cleaners had already been on that plane and the papers were most likely in the trash.

"Can we get back through security to go look on the plane ourselves, or find the cleaning crew, or go through the trash?" I desperately asked.

"I don't think so." Tammy replied, "but you can check with Delta," she said as she pointed to the ticketing counter.

Michelle at Delta was also incredibly kind and empathetic, but said it was not possible to get back through security without a ticket. I knew that if I could just beg the cleaning crew face-to-face, we'd have a chance. But by this time, Michelle shared, they probably had moved on to other planes and the papers would be buried in one of many icky trash bags. Wanting to help, Michelle jumped on the phone asking the same questions as Tammy did and getting all the same responses. They had checked the plane. No papers. They were long gone and in the trash.

Just as she was giving us the bad news, she spotted a cleaning crew walking down the corridor behind us. Like the Flash, she bolted out from behind the counter and chased after them. She found out that *they* were the crew that cleaned *our* plane! What are the chances?! However, they told her they had cleaned others after, and the multiple trash bags were already in the dumpster. I made a beeline for the crew thinking if they saw our sad faces, it might help our cause. They told us there was no way we would be allowed to dig through the trash, and they were not allowed to do so either.

I maintained my puppy dog face, and one guy showed a little empathy and said, "I'll see what we can do." The other three hesitantly followed him, none of them looking at all thrilled to be helping with our crazy problem. Staying in character like little puppy dogs, we followed them to a door and watched them go inside. We waited outside the closed door, praying fervently. After five very, very long minutes, the door slowly opened and one of them walked out. I looked at his face first to get a read. Nothing.

But was that something I saw in his hand? He held Craig's highlighted papers—a tad crumpled, but not a single sheet missing! Halleluiah! I could hear the angels rejoicing! Oh, wait, that was just Craig. We tried to give the guys cash as a thank you, but they refused. (I'm sure tipping the airplane-cleaning crew was against the rules too.) They also politely refused the cheese balls I offered, but at least one of them ended up finding me and following me on social media later that night!

We raced back to testify to the other team players, Tammy and Michelle, giving God credit and thanking them for their help. We went on to have a fabulous weekend with over 700 teenagers. The messages were received very well! We also stopped by to see Michelle on Sunday before we flew out to give her a report of the weekend. She told us we made her day and has since found me online and left a sweet message.

As I think about the effort expended to find those lost papers, and how miraculous it was that we did get our hands on them, I am reminded of the parables Jesus told in Luke 15. First, He tells about a shepherd who left ninety-nine of his sheep to go find the one lost one. Then He talks about a woman who turned her house upside down to find a lost coin. Finally, He shares about a rebellious and foolish son who ran away from home only to be greeted with joy and compassion by his father upon his return.

Jesus tells not one, not two, but three stories all with the same meaning. I think it's safe to say He wants us to understand that He will go to great lengths to find what (or who) is lost. And when He does, two verses in that chapter record that there is indeed great rejoicing in Heaven (Luke 15:7,10). Maybe that really was a choir of angels I heard rejoicing at the airport!

God's Word says... "So he got up and went to his father. But while he was still a long way off, his father saw him and was filled with compassion for him; he ran to his son, threw his arms around him and kissed him." (Luke 15: 20)

Let's Talk to God...

God,

Thank You for caring enough about me to search me out when I go astray. Please allow me to understand Your love and compassion so I am not tempted to wander. Thank You for going to such great lengths to prove Your love to me! *Amen.*

It's Your Turn!

Craig and I were just about ready to give up on those notes that were lost in the airport garbage. Is there something in your life you are ready to give up on or have already given up on? It's not too late to entrust your lost dream or desire to God. He doesn't tire of hearing from you. Maybe just writing it down will help jumpstart your faith and talk to God about it. Go ahead. He's ready and waiting.

Chapter 15

Feline Fiasco

IF YOU ARE A CAT LOVER, you will *love* this chapter. If you
despise cats, you will also love this chapter, but for a different and
twisted reason; a large part of it focuses on the downfall of my
furry friend. So, while the cat lovers will be crying, others will be
laughing. (I will try not to be mad at those people.)

I had been married only a few months, and one fall day, I
found myself feeling a little lonely. I was never lonely when my
hubby was home, but when he went to work, I was left alone in a
six-bedroom church partridge. Oh. I'm sorry. I misspelled that.
Not a partridge, a parsonage—a home provided by our church
since my husband was employed as the youth pastor. And there
was no pear tree.

I had moved from the bustling city of Minneapolis to a small
town where it was not abnormal to share the road with Amish
buggies. The entire town was smaller than the church I had been
attending. People at my new church were friendly, but I didn't
really know any of them yet, so I asked God to send me a cat to

keep me company. I told God I knew I couldn't keep it because Craig was allergic. *But God, if you could just send one to visit me now and then, that would be great,* I prayed.

I had truly *just* uttered that prayer when I walked from our kitchen to our living room. My eyes caught some movement out the big picture window, and I had to squeeze them tight and reopen them to make sure I was seeing correctly. I watched a cat walk across the street, up our driveway, and make a left turn onto our sidewalk. By the time I reached the front door, there she was—my new friend, sent directly from God, with rush shipping nonetheless!

I gave her milk; she gave me affection. I didn't take her inside, however, as tempted as I was! Not long after this meeting, I had to leave for a speaking retreat. While gone, my husband sent me a text and said, "I'm petting a cat." Aware of my husband's allergies and his *disdain* for the feline line, I thought this was a joke. Nope. My sweet sacrificial servant of a husband told me he dug deep and was nice to the cat in hopes it would come back again and pay me a visit.

She did! Again. And again. And again. And...well, she kind of started to live in our garage. And I might have sawed out part of the garage door and installed a cat flap for Jamie. Oh yeah—I named her Jamie in honor of my orange and white childhood cat named James. And then I may have, quite possibly, prayed that she would have kittens. *Wouldn't that be fun?!* I conversed with God.

I guess He agreed, because a few months later, four cute kittens were born in our garage! I actually had no idea Jamie was pregnant until the kittens appeared. Surprise! I had just assumed she had plumped up to withstand the cold Minnesota winter.

I named the two orange kittens Colby and Cheddar. And naturally, the white ones were named Mozzarella and Swiss. I became their second mother as I spent nearly every waking hour in the garage. As they grew, so did their accommodations. Initially, they kept to one small box, but when they started walking, I expanded their living quarters to just that—a quarter of the garage. Somehow by ten weeks, their cardboard compound took up over half the garage, and we could no longer park our car in there. The car wasn't the only thing staying out of the garage. So was Craig. Sadly, it was confirmed that he was allergic to the kittens.

You can imagine my total surprise when one day, *Craig* opened our front door and invited Jamie to come inside. "What?!" I questioned him.

"Well, I thought she might like a break from her kittens," Craig empathetically answered. Pitter-patter went my heart for my sweet husband.

"But what about your allergies?" I inquired.

"Maybe you should pray they go away," he suggested.

I wasn't sure if he was joking or not, but I'm not one to pass up prayer. So I laid hands on my hubby and prayed that God would take away Craig's allergies.

If I'm honest, it was a half-hearted prayer. I've had faith for much bigger things, and I had already accepted that I couldn't have Craig *and* a cat. If God's answer was dependent on my faith, Craig would have continued sneezing and wheezing whenever he was around a cat.

But…

Craig hasn't been allergic to cats since the day I prayed! Can you believe it? It would appear that God's answer had more to do with *His* desire to fulfill one of *my* desires. We found homes for the four cheeses, I mean kittens, and Jamie officially became *our* indoor cat. She lived eight great years with us. She helped us welcome both our kids into the family and was incredibly patient with our son who handled her like a ragdoll.

Jamie developed a tumor in her jaw which eventually impeded eating. The night before she was to be put down, my daughter said, "When Jamie dies, can we digest her?" I didn't know if I should laugh or cry at the disturbing comment. But then I realized my science-loving daughter meant to say, "Can we dissect her?" Is that slightly better?

My son's goodbye went something like this. He cradled her chubby cheeks (one bulging more than the other) in his tiny hands, looked into her eyes and said, "Jamie, tomorrow, you will die."

We intended to have a nice long break before considering another cat. But a trip to the Animal Humane Society steered us astray. Actually, it steered us *to* a stray. His name was Hulk, like the superhero. Isn't that incredible?! Seriously. That was his name, which helped win Craig over. At only nine months old, this gray, striped cat won our hearts.

Hulk could not have been a better cat. He snuggled. He came when he was called. He would go across the street to the park and playground with us. He even let me wear him, yes—*wear* him, in a baby carrier! He would fetch—just like a dog! And, like Jamie, he tolerated my son's violent handling. Tal's "petting" and "snuggling" consisted of wrestling and choke holds.

Hulk joined the kids for homeschooling and kept them company as they read on our giant Lovesac. In case you have yet to experience the luxury of one, allow me to paint a picture. Imagine a giant fluffy-but-firm cotton ball, six-feet wide and encased in soft fabric. As you fall backward into this plush piece of furniture, your body is cushioned and caressed on every side, leaving you in a state of total relaxation.

When Hulk claimed it as his giant cat bed, it had already been in the family for over ten years and came with lots of memories attached. Among other things, the kids used it as their landing pad for all things ninja and gymnastics. One day, after

Tal landed a perfect flip on the Lovesac, he came away with a wet bottom. Feeling very sure he did not wet himself during his flip, he came to show me. I just about lost control of myself (OK, I did lose control) when my nose confirmed my deepest fear. Urine. It *was* urine, but not my son's urine. It was CAT URINE!!!

I think I skipped all sixteen steps as I flew down the staircase. I made a pee-line, I mean a beeline, for the Lovesac. My mind raced with scenarios better than the one I suspected. *Maybe Tal was lying face down on it and Hulk jumped up and peed directly on Tal's bottom. Or maybe my son was playing a joke on me and took off his pants, rubbed them in the cat litter box, put them back on and is just pretending that Hulk peed on the Lovesac.* I soon discovered my hopeful scenarios were nothing but nonsense.

There it was. Cat pee. And lots of it.

After staring distraughtly for about ten seconds, I pinched myself to make sure it wasn't a dream. Nope. It was a nightmare, and a real one. Cat pee does NOT come out of stuff. I know this. People who don't even own cats know this.

I called my husband at work and spouted off a non-sensical explanation of what just happened. I expected him to ditch his pastoral duties immediately and come save the day. Clearly his priorities were different than mine because he said, "I'll help when I get home later. Don't do anything without me."

I pretended I didn't hear that last part and went into mission-save-the-Lovesac mode. The cover was clearly soaked, but that I could wash or even replace. The expensive fluffy filling, on the other hand, couldn't be washed and needed to be saved ASAP. *If I could remove all the filling before the cat pee soaked through the cover, maybe we'd be ok,* I thought.

So, I made what turned out to be one of the dumbest decisions I've ever made in my life. But at that moment in time, it seemed like a great idea. I raced upstairs and into our garage to gather our ten-foot by five-foot inflatable kiddie (kitty?!) pool. I nearly tripped down the stairs as I hauled this massive heap of plastic and the corded air mattress pump behind me. Thump, thump, thump, down the steps it went.

I inflated the kiddie pool in our basement guestroom, frantically throwing things aside and out of the way as this giant pool took shape. Then I raced back to the Lovesac and dragged, with all my might, the seventy-five-pound ball through three rooms and two doorways. To do the latter, I became a human battering ram as I launched myself at the Lovesac over and over again until it squeezed through each door. All the while, I was trying not to let the cat pee part touch any of the carpet, walls, or myself.

When I finally got it in the guestroom, I was so winded, I considered using the blower to inflate my lungs, but there was no time. I needed to empty out all the contents of the Lovesac into the kiddie pool and determine if it had been infiltrated with cat pee. My son, only six at the time, and clearly much wiser than me, watched me dump out heaps upon heaps of foam while shaking his head. "Mom", Tal said, "This is the worst idea you've ever had."

But there was no turning back; I was in too deep now. Literally. The foam was up to my knees as I waded through the filling. I grabbed handful after handful of material and took an extended inhalation to test if it had been compromised. My expression soured and my heart sank as my nose told me the truth. The foam had been jeopardized. It smelled like cat urine.

Now I had a huge, smelly mess on my hands—and my face since I had literally stuck my nose in cat pee. It was at this point I remembered my husband's last words on the phone. "Don't do anything without me." Oops.

As I stared at the swimming pool full of foam tainted with cat pee, I realized that my next big task was to get all that filling out of that basement room, up the stairs, outside, and into the garbage. This would have been a lot easier if I had left it intact and hauled it outside to the garbage. Each piece of shredded foam was no bigger than a mini-marshmallow, and most of the pieces weren't even half that size. Like I said earlier, this was a dumb decision!

I ran to get a lawn bag and frantically started scooping. This was going to take F-O-R-E-V-E-R! But I couldn't stop. I needed to fix this feline fiasco before my hubby came home. I was about halfway through bagging the first batch when the door slowly creaked open. There stood my husband in the doorway, lips straight, eyebrows raised, and head shaking side to side. As he looked at his wife wading in the spoiled remains of our beloved Lovesac, his signature smirk appeared. He was still shaking his head...but at least I got a grin!

And that's not all I got. My gracious husband jumped right in (cannon ball!) and started helping me take care of *my* mess. What a guy. After filling two huge garbage bags, our backs were aching, and it looked like we'd made no progress. *There must be another way.* I began to brainstorm.

And then I got a brilliant idea. Well, I'll let you be the judge of that. I ditched my husband and was back in a flash with the leaf blower from our garage. I hooked up a heavy-duty lawn bag

to the output and switched the button to sucking mode. But I
didn't press power until Craig was ready to capture this epic moment on video. 3-2-1…

KAPOW!

The leaf blower had done its job of sucking up an entire bag
of foam in less than two seconds flat, but the bag, which wasn't
heavy duty after all, burst under pressure. The room was now
a snow globe with cat-pee-soaked foam falling from the sky. It
was EVERYWHERE in our guest room—stuck to the ceiling, the
walls, and my hair. This was a total cat-astrophe!

Craig announced a standing veto on any future "brilliant ideas," so we were back to laborious bagging. Three hours and nineteen bulging bags later, we were done. Well mostly. Actually, we weren't done at all. We still had to haul the bags upstairs and outside and then dispose of them one at a time in our garbage bin over the next few months. Oh yeah, and then there was all the foam that was still plastered to every surface and piece of fabric in the guest room. Little did I know then that I'd still be finding rogue pieces of foam years later.

I fully realize that at this point, most normal, rational people would accept the death of the Lovesac. I, on the other hand am, well, not exactly normal. I spent hours researching the best concoctions to remove cat urine from fabric and worked my magic on the cover. It went through the wash cycle about ten times with every cleaning enzyme and essential oil that exists. I was quite confident I removed every trace of cat pee, and now it was time to track down comfy stuffing at an affordable price.

I was relieved to find a company willing to sell me seventy-five pounds of foam for under $100 and was thrilled when the three bulging boxes arrived at our house. We had a ton of fun as a family re-stuffing the Lovesac. It was no small task, but worth every effort when we all did a synchronized trust fall into the fluffy goodness.

After christening our refurbished favorite piece of furniture with celebratory somersaults, our cat joined the party and reclaimed his bed. I watched him like a hawk for the first few hours, but eventually relaxed, truly believing the incident was a fluke. Oh, how I wish I was right. But the next morning, he had done it again! Hulk didn't even wait twenty-four hours; how dare he!

At this point I wanted to stuff the cat in the Lovesac and roll it out the door. But instead, we stuffed the soiled sac back through several doorways, rolled it through a hallway, heaved it up the stairs and into the garage. It sat there for four months until our city held its "free bulky item pickup day," and we hauled it to the curb.

Speaking of curbs, I wanted to kick the cat to it. But Hulk's snuggles and purrs wooed me once again. Now that the Lovesac was gone, he returned to using his litter box. That is until I discovered cat urine on the guestroom pillowcase (while the guest was still staying at our house!). Don't worry, I immediately threw out the case *and* the pillow! But unfortunately, this was not an isolated incident as we soon learned he had marked his territory on the bedding of other guests staying at our house.

After a trip to the vet to rule out a bladder infection, we had to make the difficult decision to rehome Hulk. Clearly, he thought he was a dog claiming his territory, and could claim his territory in our home no more. I'm making light of it now, but at the time, it was heart-wrenching for the kids and me. I was in tears when I asked if Craig, who was silently rejoicing at the thought of a pet-free home, would pray over the situation. He prayed for our comfort, for a good home for Hulk, and for confirmation that we were making the right decision.

Not even five minutes later I was in our front yard when I noticed an officer walking across the street from the park toward my neighbor's driveway. I asked the officer if there was a problem, and he immediately pointed at Hulk who was lounging in our neighbor's yard. "Do you know whose cat that is?" he asked just before identifying himself as an animal control officer.

"Yes, it's our cat," I said. *But not for long,* I thought as I felt the tears well up.

"Well," he continued, "this cat was just seen in the park across the street, and that's illegal. This city has a leash law for any pets off your property."

I wasn't sure if I should laugh or cry. I wanted to laugh at the thought of our cat on a leash, and I wanted to cry over what felt like a punch to the gut when I was already down. But then it occurred to me that the timing of this could not be a coincidence. We had lived in this house for six years, and both Jamie and Hulk had freely roamed the neighborhood and park countless times without any run-ins with the authorities. (That sentence felt really funny to write. My cats having a problem with the law! Ha!)

Craig had *just* prayed that God would confirm if we've made the right decision, and *now* here's animal control in our front yard. Hulk spent as much if not more time outside than inside, so I knew there was no way we could limit him to the house. This officer morphed into an angel before my eyes as I recognized God's perfect timing.

God continued to awe me. A few weeks before we officially decided to send Hulk packing, I was venting to my friend, Christine, and jokingly suggested she take him to live on the hobby farm her family was about to move to. I was honestly kidding at the time, but it turned out my friend had actually given it some thought and prayer. Like Craig, she really didn't like cats but had already planned on getting at least one kitten simply because she knew how useful they can be on a farm. However, she made it clear that any cat of hers would have to be exclusively outdoors.

The family needed a few weeks to get settled in their new home which gave us time for a long goodbye and gave me time to build the mother of all outdoor cat shelters. I struggled thinking of Hulk weathering a brutal Minnesota winter outdoors, so this would be my parting gift to him and help me sleep at night knowing he was warm and cozy.

When it was completed, the beast weighed nearly 100 pounds, was double insulated, had a loft, carpeted floors, and framed pictures of our family. Oh—and we wrote personal messages to Hulk on the walls. My husband's message was especially touching. "Bye, Love Craig."

When we pulled into our friends' driveway, we noticed a huge chalk sign that sweet twelve-year-old Emma had written: "Welcome Home, Hulk!" They gave us all the time we needed to acclimate Hulk to his new home and introduce him to his new kitten buddy named Stripes. Christine decided to house the cats inside an unused chicken coop, so now they'd be doubly warm!

Driving away was sad, but we knew we could make the forty-five-minute drive and visit him in the future (which we have done many times!). Christine reported that the cats stayed up all night catching mice and became fast friends. I loved receiving picture and video updates, but soon noticed pictures of her snuggling with Hulk. *What?* I thought. *Christine doesn't like cats. What is going on?* Not only did I notice pictures of her and Hulk looking like best buddies, I noticed some of the pictures were taken *inside* her house!

Turns out Christine never knew she had a Hulk-sized hole in her heart. Unfortunately, the timing of Hulk's entrance coincided closely with the exit of her beloved husband, Josh, who had died a year earlier from cancer. Josh was an incredible husband and father, firefighter, and Navy veteran. He had an infectious smile and would light up the room.

While Josh was here, Christine would never have described herself as liking or needing touch from others. But since he's been gone, she has noticed a void which Hulk has helped fill. I've received countless pictures of Christine and Hulk snuggled up against each other, cheek to cheek, nose to nose. My sadness  is eased, and my heart is so happy, knowing Hulk is serving a purpose much greater than if he were still with our family peeing on our furniture and pillows.

I have especially loved hearing that Hulk goes on morning walks with Christine (no leash required on a hobby farm!) and sits with her while she reads the Bible and prays. I'll take credit for raising Hulk to be holy!

My kids have asked me if they think God *made* Hulk pee in our house so he would end up at Christine's farm. I can't answer that with certainty, but I can confidently echo the words from Romans 8:28 that says, "God works all things together for the good of those who love Him." I believe that when we went to the Animal Humane Society to adopt our sweet Hulky Bulky, God knew He was gifting us with a cool cat for a season before blessing Christine with a cuddly and comforting companion. Hulk will never come close to easing Christine's pain from losing her husband, but he is a reminder that God sees and cares and comforts.

As for me, I went almost a whole year without a cat before getting our cute and current kitty who is sleeping between my legs as I write this sentence. Truth be told, that year was the hardest of my life—for other reasons I wish I could expound on. Never was there a time in my life when I could use more cat snuggles, but Hulk was miles away comforting Christine. So many times, I would have buried my face in fur if there was any available. Hulk's departure made room for me to seek comfort from Christ.

After the first seven months with no pets (the longest I'd gone in over ten years), I came across two parakeets being sold at a garage sale. That was a red flag I missed. Who sells two parakeets at a garage sale!? They were extremely pretty and very quiet, so I bought them.

The minute we walked in our front door, the birds found their voices, and they didn't stop squawking until I walked them straight out the front door three days later. Don't worry, I found a very good home for them. Nature. Just kidding. Really, I'm kidding. They were rehomed with a family who somehow actually enjoys the ear piercing, headache-inducing, worse-than-nails-on-a-chalkboard sound.

Getting rid of the birds was not easy, however, because somehow, in just seventy-two hours, my kids had grown attached to these noisy creatures. The only way out, I deemed, was to promise a kitten in exchange for the birds. I kept my word, and a few months later we adopted Sprite. It was only natural to name him that since he was the replacement for the parakeets, Lemon and Lime.

You may or may not be a fan of cats, but I do hope this feline fiasco (with a couple parakeets joining the storyline at the end) has added to your admiration of God. It reminds me that He is a good Father who delights in giving good gifts (Matthew 7:11). But here's the catch—the verse finishes by saying, "to those who ask Him." So, have you asked God for anything lately? Maybe now is a good time. And if it's comfort you need, I couldn't be any more confident that God is ready and willing to deliver on that promise.

> **God's Word says...** "Praise be to the God and Father of our Lord Jesus Christ, the Father of compassion and the God of all comfort, who comforts us in all our troubles, so that we can comfort those in any trouble with the comfort we ourselves receive from God." (2 Corinthians 1:3-4)

Let's Talk to God...

God,

Thank You for being a good Father who is compassionate and comforting. As You have comforted me, please give me opportunities to be a source of comfort to others. Please open my eyes to see the gifts You have given and give me faith to ask for more. *Amen.*

It's Your Turn!

Is there anyone in your life that could use some comfort right now? Does that question sound familiar? I asked you a similar one ten chapters ago, but that person is pretty important, and they're worth me giving you a reminder! So...have you followed through with reaching out? Here are some ideas to bring comfort and care:

- Give them a call

- Send them a text

- Pass on a Scripture verse that has helped you

- Put a card in the mail

- Give them your cat (You know I'm joking, right? *Or am I?*)

- Pray for them in person

- Mow their lawn

- Clean their house (I'll take you up on that!)

- Drop off a meal

- Bring them flowers

- Watch their kids

- Take them out to coffee

- Pass on this book—now that's a GREAT idea!

What other ideas come to mind?

Closing

A God Story in Progress

YOU DID IT! Thank you! You read a lot of sentences (many more than three!), and I hope you've been encouraged. By the time this book goes to print (which I realize already happened if you are reading this!) I'm quite certain there will be more stories to add. I know this because God never stops working and life never stops happening. And guess what. You have stories too!

At the time of writing this (in my reclining chair with my cat, Sprite, schlepped across my leg) there is a God story in the making. This is a tough one, though. The toughest yet. Most of it is pretty ugly, actually. Heartbreaking to be honest. Messy and tangled. I am praying prayers that God isn't seeming to answer—at least not in the way I am hoping. I have cried a lot of tears over the last couple years, so many that when God nudged me to write this book, I rebutted with "Are you serious, God? Now? You know what I'm dealing with, right?"

It's not the right timing for me to tell you this story, but it is being written, and I am still praying. I'm also learning that when I don't know what to pray, I can pray the four powerful words Jesus modeled in Matthew 6:10: "Your will be done." As always, God's timing is just right. Instead of focusing on my fears and this current situation, God has asked me to do something quite simple.

Remember.

In writing these stories down, I have remembered that God is faithful in hard times. I remember that He sees me. I remember that He comforts me. I remember that He speaks to me. I remember that He listens to me. I remember that He is personable. I remember that His ways are better than my ways. I remember that beauty can come from brokenness.

And here I thought God was asking me to write this book for Him! But the reality is, it's been for me…and for you! This isn't the first time God has asked His people to remember. Time and time again God asked the Israelites to remember His miracles, His faithfulness, and His goodness. He asked them to recount the wonders to their children and grandchildren. He instructed them to make a conscious effort to remember because He knows how easily we forget.

Now that I've shared my stories, it's your turn! Would you consider recounting and recording the God stories in your life? I actually have a running list on my phone titled "God Stories" so I can quickly record them as they happen and as I remember. If nothing immediately comes to mind, pause and pray. Watch and listen.

I know that the Lord is working in your life, and there are countless God stories in the making. God desires to write an epic story with all the parts of your life—the good, the bad, the embarrassing (think urine-infused foam stuck to the ceiling), and yes, even the ugly. We do have an enemy, however, and he wants a say in our story. He'd like to make some edits, additions, and deletions. He'd like it if you didn't remember the God stories. But here's the good news—you decide who holds the pen. And if you pick God, He writes His stories with permanent ink!

So be encouraged, my friend. God is in the details of your life, and He wants to bless you. Pray about the big things. Pray about the little things. The more you pray, the more you will notice where and how He is working. Your God story is in progress!

God's Word says..."...He who began a good work in you will carry it on to completion until the day of Christ Jesus." (Philippians 1:6)

Let's Pray...

God,

Would You bring to my memory times in which You've shown up in my life? Remind me of Your faithfulness. Help me recall what You've done. Please open my eyes to the opportunities to share these stories with others and give me the courage to testify of Your goodness. *Amen.*

It's Your Turn!

Did you think you were done? Not quite! Now that you've read fifteen of my God stories, I have to imagine that some of yours have been brought to memory. Here's your chance to start a list; I've even numbered it for you.

Write down a word or two or your own clever title to each story of God's faithfulness in your life.

1.

2.

3.

4.

5.

6.

7.

8.

9.

10.

11.

12.

13.

14.

15.

But please don't keep your list confined to this book—share it! Before you close this book, determine who you will share these stories with—a friend, a family member, a neighbor, the delivery person, me?

Yes—me! At the very least, would you take a picture of page 196 after you write down your God story titles and send it to me? You can message me on social media @cheeseballchick or through www.cheeseballchick.com. It would make me smile SO big! Better yet, write out your whole God story and send it to me! Because now it's *my* turn to hear *your* stories! Ready, GO!

Acknowledgements

SINCE THIS IS A BOOK of God stories, it's only fitting and fair to thank God first and foremost. *He* is the reason this book came to be. Thank you, Lord, for Your creativity, kindness, compassion, humor, and personal involvement in my life. And thanks for helping me pull this book off—wow! Wouldn't and couldn't have done it without You!

I am also so thankful for my best friend and hubby, Craig, for all the late nights of reading and re-reading these stories. Thank you for being my biggest (and most handsome) cheerleader!

Thank you, Heidi Sheard (HS), for going above and beyond what most editors do and helping me with *all* parts of this book. The very best thing you did was consult with God. I LOVE that you prayed for His wisdom as you edited. Thank YOU for doing the most important thing—talking to the ultimate Author!

To the other Heidi, Heidi Koopman (HK)—thank you for your commitment to Christ and your commitment to excellence from cover to cover. And thank you for coming through in the eleventh hour—*you* are another God story!

Ali, Mandy, Sawyer, and Niles—thank you for helping create and capture the fun cover photos! I haven't laughed that hard in a long time!

Thank you to my friends and family (you know who you are!) for reading, brainstorming, and praying with me. I am beyond grateful for all the camps, churches, schools, and conferences who have invited me in to speak and given me a platform to share God stories over the last twenty years.

And I surely cannot forget Home Depot Jim. Thank you for using your creativity and problem-solving skills to help me create the cheese ball dispenser. Would you have ever guessed that the simple phrase "How can I help you?" would put you in a book?!

Finally, to YOU—the reader. Thank you for the time you've invested in this book. It makes my heart happy. THE END.

About the Author

BESIDES CARRYING SNACKS on her back, Molly Sanborn is a proud wife, a homeschool mom, and a speaker from Minneapolis, Minnesota. She speaks at youth and women's events and loves tag-team speaking with her husband, Craig, to teens and adults. The Sanborns count it a privilege to partner with FamilyLife as communicators for the Weekend to Remember marriage conferences. Molly spent a year with Youth With A Mission (YWAM) in their Discipleship Training School which included mission work in China, Turkey, and Mexico. She has a bachelor's degree in elementary education from North Central University and a master's degree in marriage and family therapy from Liberty University. She uses it mostly to counsel her husband to listen to her point of view. When not on the road speaking or handing out cheese balls, you can find Molly on a ninja course with her kids training for their next competition or exploring God's great creation.

Socials: @cheeseballchick
Online: www.CheeseBallChick.com

Looking for a speaker for an upcoming event?

NOW THAT YOU'VE MET ME, can I meet you?! I'd love to speak at your next event and give you some cheese balls! I enjoy speaking to all ages and stages and can craft messages to meet a specific theme or event—teens, women, mother-daughter, etc. Some of my most requested talks are: "Overwhelmed to Overflowing," "Obsessive Comparison Disorder," "The Constant Conversation" (about prayer), "Playful Parenting," "Keep Your Pants On!" and of course—"Cheese Balls for Jesus!" My style is pretty much like how I write—comical, practical, and biblical. *Request more information at **cheeseballchick.com***

As much as I like speaking solo, I *love* speaking with my husband, Craig. We speak to teens, young adults, families, parents, and couples. Our most requested talk for teens is called, "Lessons from a Love Story." At marriage events, we love to share "Cha-Ching—The Art of Investing in Your Marriage" and "Remember and Rekindle." *Request more info at **CraigandMolly.com***

Made in the USA
Monee, IL
27 September 2022